# SUCCESS BY DESIGN

## REVEALING PROFILES OF CALIFORNIA ARCHITECTS

### JENN KENNEDY

*Jenn Kennedy*

**kennedy pix**

Produced for publisher by

Sea Hill Press, Inc.
Santa Barbara, California
www. seahillpress.com

Production Manager: Greg Sharp
Book Designer: Judy Petry
Editor: Gina Z. Terlinden

Published 2011
Printed in Hong Kong

ISBN 978-0-9830771-0-7

# Dedication

Thank you to the many people who helped me along the way, beginning with Stephen Kanner, who sat for an interview, made introductions, and shepherded this project through the early stages. I also want to thank all of those who brainstormed late night, reviewed drafts and designs, and offered advice and support of all stripes—specifically thank you to Andrea, Dad, Elisa, Emily, Georgene, Gina, Greg, Kayce, Mandy, Michael, Michele, Michelle, Mom, Sherry, and Tibbie. It took a village.

# Introduction

## by Jenn Kennedy

A successful architectural career is the result of many factors, including education, design, proficiency, and simple luck. Staring down the barrel of an imminent recession, I wondered how businesses survive—and even thrive—through market downturns, natural growing pains, and inherent business challenges such as staffing, marketing, and client relations.

Through this project, I set out to speak to architects who have either started their own successful firms or have senior partner positions at large, well-known firms. I chose twenty-five architects from all over California who have a range of specialties, including residential, education, hospitality, retail, and civic, and I asked these innovators about their beginnings, mentors, mistakes, and lessons learned. They opened up to me about highlights and low points of their journey.

This book offers stories of many diverse paths to success for those interested in starting or managing an architecture practice. All licensed, California-based architects, my subjects were interviewed and photographed in the same session.

# Contents

# Foreword

In *Success by Design*, I am extremely glad to find that Jenn Kennedy's collection of successful California architects goes beyond Frank Gehry and Thom Mayne.

California is not a place where landmarks command. It is a place that organizes things horizontality in a rather anonymous fashion—points and dots whose banality evolves and regenerates both formality and vitality. The meaning of architecture emerges from connecting the points, and the role of architects is to traverse the dots.

This survey and its stories lie exactly in the contours of Los Angeles. Despite the overall feeling of excessive modern nostalgia, one can detect a few strands of fresh sights—interiorized spatiality, monolithic materiality, and temporary permanence—to name a few that stay out of the L.A. clichés. One might be curious as to how these strands can be knitted to fill the void left in L.A. and California, post-Morphosis.

"Success" in my mother tongue does not mean capacity realized; it means realizing ability—in other words, the potentiality to become something else. The vividness and variety of this group fits well in my language of success.

As an educator, I am deeply impressed by the different routes by which each individual architect has achieved his or her success. Together, they have manifested how architectural education prepares students to take diverse trajectories in their careers and lives.

Qingyun Ma
Dean
Della & Harry MacDonald Chair
University of Southern California School of Architecture

Barry Berkus

(Jenn Kennedy)

# BARRY BERKUS, AIA, President
# Berkus Design Studio

Barry Berkus is synonymous with Santa Barbara. Between his teaching, speaking circuit, impressive career, and cycling club, everyone seems to know him. I met him at his downtown home, which emulates his energetic soul. It's a minimal and modern loft—decorated solely in black, white, and red—but comfortable and populated with items that say he's a thinking, adventurous man. His high-end road bicycle sits beneath a giant color portrait of his acquaintance, Lance Armstrong, just one piece of his expansive art collection that's housed in the airy loft where he and his wife Jo have hosted fund-raisers for museums and have had numerous fireside chats with notable thinkers, philanthropists, athletes, and creatives.

During his twenties to forties, Berkus set world records in hydroplaning, skied the Rockies (via helicopter drops), climbed in the Antarctic, and skippered six transpacific yacht races. Because of his curious spirit, he can hold a conversation with just about anyone. "I can sit down with anybody and talk about what they love, regardless of whether it's art, sailing, biking, etcetera," he says. "You have to be interesting beyond just your profession and be able to communicate so people enjoy being with you as well as know you're good at what you do." Also a voracious reader, he devours books on new urbanism, economics, social issues, and current events.

Berkus began college with a focus on economics but realized early on that he did not enjoy it. He always loved to draw, so he went back to Glendale Community College, earned straight As, and transferred to the architecture school at the University of Southern California (USC). "It was exciting and I knew I'd found my place," he says.

With a desire to leave a legacy, Berkus pursued housing work—a specialty other architects didn't want to do. He explains that during the 1950s and '60s, most architects thought housing was beneath them. "They wanted to design edifices, but I had a goal to change the way housing looked," he explains. "I wanted to give it a sculpted feeling, an innovative component to nurture people. I strived to use volume, light, and shapes. And eventually, when I was working for someone else part-time, I got to a point when I knew I could do it better on my own." Housing also appealed to Berkus because he thought he could reach more people and change the way they perceived space—even the way they looked at life and how they nurtured their family. "I had a greater mission," he says.

While at USC, Berkus worked part-time for L.C. Major, one of the most active housing designers in California. At only twenty-one years old, Berkus was offered a high-level management position, his own office, and an $800-per-month salary, which seemed like the world to him. While the promise of a stable income appealed to him and his young wife, Gail, they decided against it. In a lucky turn of events, Major's firm eventually consolidated and as a result, could no longer service its clients in the area. Berkus didn't hesitate to start his own business, initially with a partner, to fill the gap left by his previous employer.

While it was never a goal to grow a big office, soon he had twenty people on staff. He cites his projects getting published as the element that really fueled the growth but also insists that they were published without any effort on his part. They were being published because his company was doing something different that got noticed by the building, design, and planning communities—they were filling a void. He remembers some people smirked at these builders because they did tract homes, but Berkus saw himself as a pioneer. He completed projects for Bill Levitt (*Time* named him the "Creator of Suburbia"), US Homes, and Arthur Rutenberg because they wanted to change the way they were doing housing, and Berkus had a reputation as being the architect to do it.

Then came requests to design projects in New York, Washington, DC, Miami, and other cities. When Berkus Design Studio reached two hundred employees—with offices in New York, Miami, DC, Atlanta, Chicago, Los Angeles, Orange County, San Francisco, and Tokyo—he was pressured to become licensed. As for the day-to-day oversight at the offices, Berkus hired regional managers and named one main executive in Los Angeles to whom everyone reported.

When the company went public in 1971, it began considering modular housing. In order to understand this market, Berkus provided a $20,000 grant to UC Los Angeles (UCLA) in 1968 to research data on every modular unit created up to that point. Through the research, he concluded that mobile homes were the only successful factory-built home that made money and lasted for any length of time. With this data in hand, he approached the National Association of Home Builders and said, "Let's change the way housing is built." He designed the first smart house, which included a new plug and outlet system to create an electronic tie throughout the house. This system provides improved convenience, comfort, energy efficiency, and security. Berkus also explored designing various homes on wheels.

He considers architecture a privilege. "I'm not in it for money," he says. "The responsibility and liability of practicing is not proportional to the income. You must have a love for the art. Exploring— both socially and structurally—is something all architects should do."

To initially attract clients, he built prototypes. For one client, he built full-scale cardboard houses in a warehouse to show how his idea would read. "We had to prove our thinking process without making the client take too big of a risk," he says. Years ago, when he first worked for Levitt, the houses were considered weird looking since they were not colonial or federal style, so he built them out in the forest first, then relocated them if they worked. "Everything is a collaboration," he says. "I had the best clients in the world. They had done research, and I had met with experts about the structuring of social order within a community. We knew how people bought houses. I learned this from my clients, not from school."

As for schmoosing, Berkus does play golf, but not with the intention of nurturing clients. He attends events to learn about the industry and meet new people, not necessarily to sell himself. "By pursuing my interests, I've met interesting, powerful people who sometimes become clients," he explains. He notices that architects are protective and territorial, and he hypothesizes they don't socialize with each other for fear of losing work. But he sees things differently: "I think there is room for many more architects, and I like seeing the young guard expressing themselves. It's a breath of fresh air."

"I've always gone to the far edge of the planet in my thinking," Berkus says. "I'm in my seventies now, and I've failed a bunch, in part because security never interested me." He has weathered multiple recessions, citing the 1970s oil recession as the worst. During this devastating downturn, he lost his two-hundred-person publicly held firm. "I had done well for quite a while and thought we were

Ortega Ridge
residence
(Peter Malinowski/
InSite Architectural
Photography)

UC Santa Barbara Mosher Alumni House (Jim Bartsch Photography)

invincible," he says. "Then all of a sudden, the world rolled over me. I couldn't pull back fast enough. We grew fast, and while I had a great board of directors, I didn't have any senior thinking. The market changes quickly in architecture, and it's difficult to scale up and down with it." He echoes what several other seasoned architects have discovered: "We had a lot of debt in the firm, and that will kill you," he advises. "Build with the least amount of debt. Leveraging used to be acceptable, but it's not anymore."

Another lesson Berkus learned in his fifty-plus years of business was to hire people older than him. "I didn't look for gray, which I should have—people who had been burned before and could have raised a flag when I was going in a dangerous direction or uncharted waters," he says. "Instead, I had too many people who just believed in who I was. If I could go back, I would have balanced it more."

When asked about his current recession strategy, Berkus says, "Work harder than ever to find a niche. In a recession, there is always something that hasn't been done. People need to be convinced that niche exists." He admits this recession has hit him hard: "I'm actually spending more hours working now than I did when I was thirty."

Berkus says architects—by nature—are optimists. "I've grown by taking risks and assuming it would work out," he says. "Even recently, with single-family homes in Santa Barbara, I've built them and then people buy them. I knew it was right. I believe in light and height in urban areas because the garden isn't as much a part of your environment." He attributes his success to his sense of adventure. Early on, he explored space and housing for people who didn't have great means, giving them a feeling of worth and well-being. He also cites discovering modules and working in alternative-building types— such as copper and solar—in the 1970s and '80s as a key differentiator.

Berkus has spent time at the Aspen Institute; lectures at the Massachusetts Institute of Technology (MIT), Harvard University, UC Santa Barbara, and Texas A&M University; and sits on several boards. To young or new architects, he imparts: "Have confidence in yourself. As an artist, record the time you live in and tell stories through your work." He says architects are fortunate because they leave a legacy. "Go where life takes you and run hard. Passion is what's going to take you to the other end."

Ortega Ridge residence
(Farshid Assassi)

Pacific Palisades residence, CA
(Tom Bonner Photography)

Pacific Palisades residence (Tom Bonner Photography)

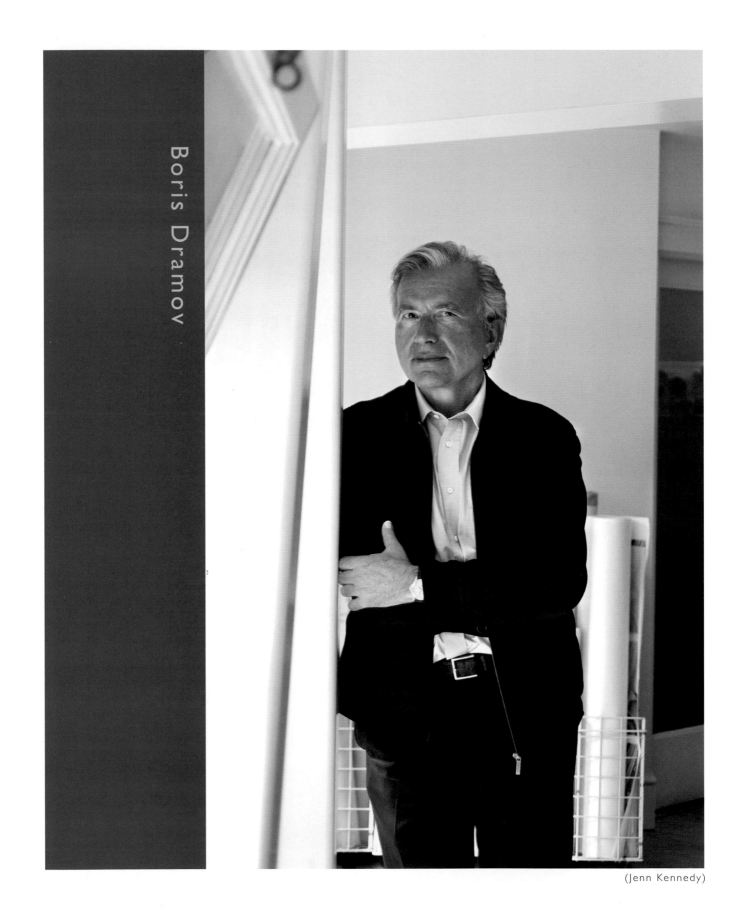

Boris Dramov

(Jenn Kennedy)

# BORIS DRAMOV, FAIA, President
# ROMA Design Group

ROMA Design Group resides in a historical, light-filled loft in the bustling North Beach neighborhood of San Francisco. Situated atop a café with street noise feeding the creative hunger, the office is distinctly noncorporate, a place where pondering the meaning of life would seem to take place first and foremost at the watercooler.

Firm president Boris Dramov is a pensive, philosophical leader. Having spent a great deal of time in the academic world, Dramov is a man of theory and great intellect. He obtained his undergraduate degree in architecture from USC, his masters of architecture from Columbia University, and attended Harvard University's Loeb Fellowship program during the social revolution of the late 1960s and early '70s. "My professors were asking provocative questions at this time, and USC had a very abstract approach to design and architecture," he recalls. "I became interested in changing society, dealing with issues of social equity, and influencing the environment."

In contrast to many architects of the day, Dramov says, "I didn't want to just build houses for wealthy people. Nor did I pursue development in the outskirts of cities." He became interested in architecture as urbanism and focused on urban infill and transforming the city fabric. Throughout his career, he has upheld a strict policy of taking only work that parallels his values, which has led him to specialize in designing urban spaces.

Dramov cites witnessing the transformation of Los Angeles during his undergraduate years as an early influence. After finishing at USC, he went to San Francisco, another city experiencing tremendous social upheaval. Dramov worked for a few architectural firms before heading to graduate school at Columbia. He felt it was important to experience both coasts and further his education in a different setting. During his time in New York, he says, "I saw a new level of urbanism and came to understand that architects can't solve every urban problem. I'm an architect, not a social worker or politician."

Dramov worked in traditional architecture throughout undergraduate and graduate school. Designing buildings with César Pelli at Victor Gruen Associates was a highlight of his career before he transferred to the firm's urban planning department. Dramov also cites his tenure at Wallace McHarg Roberts & Todd as a period of personal and creative growth. He worked with not only architects but also urbanists and landscape architects who were best known for the book *Design with Nature*. While there, he met his wife and business partner, Bonnie Fisher.

Meeting Fisher significantly influenced Dramov's career path. As a landscape architect, she was environmentally focused, which has impacted their now-thirty-year collaboration. For example, in the numerous public spaces they have designed together, Dramov says they don't differentiate between the inside and outside of a building.

ROMA Design Group was an existing firm that Dramov and Fisher eventually acquired. "We were interested in working on the waterfront project in San Francisco," Dramov explains. "ROMA got the job, so we came in as employees with the intention of becoming partners. There are a lot of good reasons to join an existing firm. There's also baggage and things we eventually changed, so it better reflected us."

While Dramov is obviously passionate about theory and concepts, he noticeably avoids questions about running the business. When asked if he feels he's a strong businessperson, he confesses, "Good enough, but not good. You do the administrative and business part because that's what is required to do what you really love. There are people who are interested in architecture as a business, but that's not me."

Because the firm kept winning projects in Austin, Texas, they opened a local office. There are three partners in the firm, but Dramov says they do not divide roles and responsibilities because they have similar skills. ROMA does, however, employ an in-house controller to oversee finances.

Dramov attributes the firm's steady workflow purely to reputation. "We don't win projects because we go to social clubs or mingle," he says. "We go after specific jobs that we know are a perfect fit. We don't pursue everything. If you want to be a twenty-five to thirty-person firm—as we are—you must define your boundaries, your target projects." And he prefers to keep to the current size, saying, "When you get beyond thirty people, casual management becomes difficult, and you must have a very structured management approach. Our firm is still able to build large projects by partnering with other firms."

Dramov and Fisher are very hands-on when it comes to the hiring—they, and other senior employees, conduct all interviews. "We're not looking for people who still want to be taught," he says. "We want people who understand how to be productive and who can add value." He wants candidates with computer skills and leadership qualities and adds, "Many people are talented and creative, but that's not enough."

ROMA doesn't have multiple studios like some firms do, but rather projects are pathed to various employees based on their specialties. "Many architects who are single practitioners or who work in small firms tend to do it all," he says. "But when you get into a larger office, people are very good at only certain things. All together, the office is really good at all of them, so any shortcomings are filled by strengths of another, and the so shortcomings are allowed to survive. One could say that's a detriment because people don't improve their shortcomings, but there are those that find a great deal of satisfaction in doing only the tasks at which they excel."

As for his favorite project, he explains logically, "You can't hang your hat on just one job. The project that seems the least interesting may turn out to be the most exciting, and the one that seems so great in the beginning sometimes brings the most difficulty and problems." Dramov points to a city planning assignment displayed on a nearby board, revealing, "This little project was exciting because it turned this small town around. While I wouldn't consider it a glamorous project, the people were great and that made all the difference."

Dramov hasn't considered a transition plan for the future. "I enjoy working, so there's no rush," he says. "Not many architects want to lead a firm. They may say they do, but are they really willing to pay the price?" Acknowledging that architecture is not a nine-to-five job, he explains, "Because Bonnie and I are married, it has worked for us. It's hard to give the amount of energy that it takes. You have to get the job, write the contract, and hire the right employees to make it profitable. Then you have to see that everyone is working creatively and appropriately. It's a lot." Dramov credits his immigrant mentality to pushing him to achieve more than others.

Clearly from a creative family, Dramov and Fisher's daughters are also pursuing architecture and industrial design. In recent years, since their kids have grown, the couple has taken more vacations, although they often still work while on retreat. "Sometimes," he says, "you have to get distance so you can see the forest through the trees."

Third Street Promenade,
Santa Monica, CA
(Jane Lidz)

Union City Intermodal Station, CA
(Christopher Grubbs)

Steven Ehrlich

(Jenn Kennedy)

# STEVEN EHRLICH, FAIA, Design Principal
## Ehrlich Architects

From the moment I entered his realm, it was apparent that Steven Ehrlich is an adventurer. His much-photographed, modern Venice, California, home reflects someone well traveled who likes to entertain. The walls open for indoor/outdoor living, and the suspended glass walkway also houses a projector for screening movies.

When I asked how he knew architecture was his path, Ehrlich jumped up and went to hunt down a photo from his seventh grade science fair project—a solar home. "I just knew," he says. "Even younger than twelve, I used to love to build forts, tree houses and lean-tos. My father was an engineer and inventor and it just evolved. I never wavered."

Ehrlich graduated from Rensselaer Polytechnic Institute in architecture in 1969, a tumultuous time. To avoid the Vietnam War draft, he decided to join the Peace Corps, a service option he believed in. He was stationed in Marrakech and worked for the Moroccan governmental housing and architecture office for two years. He learned immensely from the indigenous builders. During his stay, Ehrlich acquired both French and conversational Arabic, traveled extensively, and became more of a world citizen. "I realized that there are many ways of life, many differences, and richness in the diversity of cultures," he says.

Ehrlich learned firsthand from these accidental mentors. "When people are living in delicate balance with the Earth," he says, "they don't have a lot of outside applied muscle, like the ability to import steel from Japan. They have to build right on site." Looking back to these early builders, he says, "It's funny that everyone is embracing sustainability now, yet these people were doing it five hundred years ago. That knowledge was embedded in me from a very fundamental position." He is still interested in community-based building and cites a community center, library, or museum as his dream project.

Next, Ehrlich spent a year traveling across the Sahara and exploring several West African countries. His adventures took him from the deserts to the rainforests, where he witnessed the architectural changes responding to the environment. "I began to understand the embedded sustainable wisdom that the indigenous builders possess, and learned invaluable lessons," he says. Ehrlich knows that while much of what happened during his early career was circumstantial and out of his control, he was open to it and embraced it—an attitude that has served him well.

Ehrlich returned to the United States and worked for a Manhattan-based architect for six months during the leading edge of the SoHo loft renovations. Next, he moved to Vermont and designed and built houses with a friend for eighteen months. Africa was still calling, however, so he took a three-year position teaching architecture in Nigeria. Ehrlich looks back on his years in Africa as a very formative time. "It was a time of taking," he says. "I was taking the information, knowledge, and generosity of other cultures. When I hit thirty, something switched and I was ready to give back—both through architecture and by raising a family."

While living in Africa, Ehrlich became interested in indoor/outdoor relationships and what that meant. "Multicultural groups of people living together fascinated me," he says. After visiting his sister, who lived in a Richard Neutra house in the Hollywood Hills, he decided to relocate to California. "I liked that Los Angeles architecture wasn't based on tradition, but invited the question, 'Where do we go from here?'" He worked for two years for an architect then went out on his own on a project. Through contacts he made while building homes in Vermont, he was commissioned to design and build a home in the Santa Cruz Mountains in California. He hired a crew of craftsmen and spent a year completing the project. It was a design/build project, a delivery method he likes and sees as a growing trend.

After setting up residency in Los Angeles and passing his licensing exams, he officially launched his own business. Starting from ground zero, he jokingly called himself a specialist in closet remodels. Those closets, however, eventually led to kitchens and bathrooms, and suddenly a wing of a house or a second-story bedroom. "I had a breakthrough opportunity where I designed a studio guesthouse adjacent to a Neutra house," he recalls. "That project was photographed by Julius Schulman and caught the imagination of multiple magazines. It was on the cover of the Home section of the *New York Times*. That changed my career and opened my world."

Ehrlich recalls that postmodernism was reigning supreme, yet his projects were successfully beating to a different drum. "I had come from this primal experience in Africa and I wasn't tapped into the trends," he says. "I wanted to do my own thing." The Southern California Institute of Architecture (SCI-Arc) and UCLA also saw his talent and invited him to guest lecture and teach.

Ehrlich says, with passion and ambition, it's possible to break out of the residential sector and do public work too: "It's in our nature to try to get the next big project, to increase our sphere of influence. I always wanted a more diverse practice that embraced the public. It's not easy for a fledgling architect to move into that realm. By getting to know some of the right people, I was given an opportunity." He was chosen to design the Shatto Recreation Center for the City of Los Angeles Department of Recreation & Parks. It was an unusual design and he collaborated with Ed Moses, a well-known artist. Ehrlich admits it didn't just happen by chance: "I made a conscious effort to get to know people at various public facilities—the school district, parks department, etcetera. I was also getting published, which peaked their interest."

Early on, Ehrlich did all the office tasks on his own. He hired his first employee after two years and slowly added another. They started in his garage then moved to a larger space above his garage. Five years in, he finally rented an actual office. At this point, he had five employees, including a bookkeeper and marketing person. He was consciously building the practice slowly. "I'm the tortoise, not the hare," he explains. "I don't want to get bigger than thirty-five people. I am committed to our studio. I know every employee and their spouse. It's atelier style. And we are all in one large room together, which I like." When hiring, Ehrlich looks for people young or old, but they must possess passion for their work, good computer skills, and a compelling design portfolio.

While Ehrlich's office is located in Los Angeles, they do many projects in other locations, including Taiwan, Nigeria, Dubai, and Spain, and therefore often collaborate with local architects. "I don't see a large practice as necessary," he says. "During the last five years, I've taken on three partners. It's great to share in the governance of the practice. We have four associates who are the next generation as well. We are creative and built a society/studio. It attracts talented people who are vested. I'm not a guy in a cape, these are complex design problems that take teams."

Arizona State University Cronkite Center of Journalism (Bill Temmerman)

When asked about an exit strategy, Ehrlich says, "I'll retire when they carry me out horizontally in a box." He acknowledges that all three partners have different strengths. He explains one has experience with academic architecture, one has more technical skills, and the other is good with management and residential design. "We are all designers but with different specialties," he says. "We're complementary. I'm considered the design principal, but everyone is a designer in our firm."

Ehrlich does offer up his philosophy on client relations by saying, "I've always tried to do architecture as creatively as possible but within the paradigm of reality. For example, if I'm hired to design a house for budget X, then it's incumbent upon me to come close to that budget. If it's far beyond, it isn't fair. I have to be knowledgeable enough, sensible enough, and caring enough that I'm designing within the reality. And that's why I'm not afraid of design/build because architecture and construction go hand in hand. I say, 'Let's roll up our sleeves and make this a reality.' I don't ignore the client; in fact, I've always embraced their needs, dreams, and desires. I think it's because I've been embracing of those values that I've been successful."

From a lifestyle standpoint, he acknowledges the challenge of juggling a young family. "The only thing harder than being an architect is being married to one," he says. "It's a lot to find balance. When you are running a practice and believe in your work and you're ambitious—which I am—then that is a lot." After years in practice, his office now has the infrastructure to run for weeks at a time without him as he travels to deliver lectures or take vacations.

And what does he like most about his job today? "I'd say A to Z, with the exception of L, M, and Q, because there are a lot of steps from A to Z, but I like the end result. And I'm willing to go through all the steps. I like wearing different hats. If tested, I would have been diagnosed with ADD and dyslexia. I love shifting, refocusing, and seeing multiple projects moving forward at the same time. You have to be both patient and energetic."

Acknowledging that architecture has a slow gestation period, Ehrlich says, "Most architects don't hit full stride until they're in their fifties. I was off on a tangent during my twenties." He advises aspiring architects to be passionate, practical, and good listeners: "Don't believe in something superfluous or gratuitous. Rather, put you focus toward something that has meaning for everyone."

700 Palms residence,
Venice, CA
(Erhard Pfeiffer)

Kendall Lab
(Peter Vanderwarker)

Richard Emsiek

(Jenn Kennedy)

# RICHARD EMSIEK, AIA, President and COO
# McLarand Vasquez Emsiek & Partners

Orange County is filled with bronzed, handsome athletes. It almost seems a prerequisite for residency. Richard Emsiek is no exception. Statuesque with a broad, easy smile, he invited me on a tour of the Irvine office over which he presides.

Emsiek was raised in a family focused on aesthetic sensibilities. "Our houses were always interesting," he recalls. "I remember a home that had no dining room, even though there were five kids in our family. It had a casual great room instead, which was about forty years ahead of its time." He had several aunts and uncles in the design profession, either as interior architects or building architects. He also recalls his colorful great aunt, Alice Vanek: "Larger than life, she was the chair of architecture at a college in the Midwest. Her home was purely white except her matching dogs, which were jet black. She wore nothing but purple and told stories of her time with Frank Lloyd Wright."

At age thirteen, Emsiek decided to pursue architecture. Clearly bent toward becoming a designer, he knew early on that he was much more interested in how things looked than how they worked. He attended Cal Poly Pomona and graduated in 1981 with a bachelor of science and in 1982 with a bachelor of architecture.

Knowing he wanted to make himself more valuable to potential employers, Emsiek worked for several firms while still in college. The first was an East coast firm specializing in high rises. "I was fortunate to be taken under the wing of a very talented designer who taught me that great work begins with a well-thought-out concept, followed by thorough execution of that concept. This includes tending to even the smallest issues. He also taught that learning our craft requires paying dues and learning from everything I do."

Next, he worked for Linda Taylor, who had a small firm in Newport Beach, California. "We did everything from designing interiors to vacuuming the office," he says. He also recalls having a glass of wine every day at 4:00 pm with Taylor, who became a mentor and good friend. They designed mostly custom homes in Orange County, and then her practice evolved into designing large medical buildings, which didn't interest Emsiek. "I learned a great deal about the mechanics of things through Linda," he says, "however, it was too small of an office, and I have a short attention span." After two and a half years, he left to go to a large firm in Orange County for several years.

Recently married and looking for a firm with growth potential, he took a job in 1985 with the firm that now bears his name: McLarand Vasquez Emsiek & Partners (MVE & Partners). He worked closely with Ernesto Vasquez, one of the partners, for a number of years and eventually asked if he could run a housing development project on his own in 1987. With hesitation, Vasquez agreed, and later that year, Emsiek was promoted to associate partner, skipping the associate level. In the subsequent years, he took on a tremendous workload and managed fifteen people. He notes a significant turning point in 1988, when he started learning the business side and handling contractual negotiations. "Never in my wildest plan would I have ever wanted to do that," he says, "but it was part of the natural progression." Through this added responsibility, he became closer to Carl McLarand, the other partner, and broadened his overall skill set.

Emsiek attributes his fast track success to his ability to manage work and clients, to service the clients well, and to his design capabilities. "Pretty soon, you're taking on more work and billing a lot of money," he explains, "People notice and opportunities present themselves." At thirty-eight years old, he made partner.

Today, Emsiek has the same two partners in the business: Carl McLarand, chairman and CEO, and Ernesto Vasquez, vice president. As president and COO, Emsiek handles the day-to-day management of the firm. All three men are responsible for new business, marketing, and design. Emsiek notes that they all came up through the design side of the business. He believes the design track doesn't happen by accident and says, "You have to be very comfortable starting with a blank piece of paper, which most technical people prefer not to do. If you think of really talented technical people, their first inclination is to ask 'why?,' while designers ask 'why not?'"

The firm has expanded and contracted throughout the years. Following a late-1980s boom, it grew as large as one hundred staffers, however during the middle 1990s, a recession forced it down to thirty-five staffers. "It was so painful to do those layoffs," Emsiek says, "so we made significant management decisions to address the challenges." They instituted a four-day production workweek and diversified the business. He explains, "We were still doing commercial and residential, but we weren't doing retail or institutional. We made inroads in various market sectors and geographic locations to amortize the impact of future recessions." And while they have strategically tried to remain as recession proof as possible, he acknowledges that while they were 170 people at the end of 2007, they have again cut back to their current one hundred employees. "We're now in a global recession," he adds. "When the market's zigging, you have to zag. This means turning down some work so you don't get the highs and lows. You can never staff up big enough in the boom times and you can never downsize quick enough in the hard times."

Emsiek is adamant about quality control and would rather take fewer projects and do them well. As a result, he acknowledges that clients don't retain their firm to "bang a project out." He adds, "That's not where we've positioned ourselves fee-wise. There are plenty of firms that will take direction unilaterally—something we don't do well." That said, Emsiek acknowledges: "There's no doubt we need to get commissions consistently. We have a lot of financial obligations and mouths to feed."

Thinking about a dream project, he names a past project—the Reserve: "It was a private golf club and we're very proud of it. The site is amazing and we designed the land plan and much of the residential buildings. I think of the Reserve as a once-in-a-lifetime project, because even though the architectural part was arguably minimal, we were able to pursue an idea with a fully engaged client who said, 'Tell us what you think it should be.' There are also days when I'd love to do a cabin or design a cathedral—a space that's totally user based and not designed for economic returns."

While he considers himself exceptionally energetic, Emsiek acknowledges that balancing home and work life requires a lot of effort and patience on the part of his family. "It wasn't by accident that it has worked out," he says. "I went to as many baseball and soccer games as I possibly could, even if it meant I came back to the office later. I learned to manage my day as best as I could and closed the door when quiet time was needed."

Emsiek is a big believer in community service and asks all employees to adopt a cause. He sits on many boards, including the Orange County chapter of the Boy Scouts of America, although he never

Newport Bluffs Recreation Center,
Newport Beach, CA
(Eric Figge)

The Reserve,
Indian Wells, CA
(Eric Figge)

The Reserve
(Eric Figge)

3rd Avenue Lofts, Scottsdale, AZ (Eric Figge)

did it to solicit business. "It has to happen more naturally than that," he says. "If anybody joins an organization with the sole purpose of generating business, it's probably not going to work out well. Organizations want board members to make something happen for them." He became involved with the boy scouts because he was impressed with the mission and the Orange County Council scout executive, Kent Gibbs, whose enthusiasm and passion for the mission was infectious. MVE & Partners designed the Orange County headquarters located in Santa Ana, California, pro bono.

Emsiek doesn't show his hand regarding his future plans: "I've been fortunate to be involved in many great projects with many talented colleagues and clients, and I'll keep practicing as long as I remain excited."

Elisa Garcia

(Jenn Kennedy)

# ELISA GARCIA, President
# Garcia Architects

Sometimes it's hard to know if one has a calling or if they simply followed a familiar and well-traveled path. From her earliest memories, Elisa Garcia always wanted to be an architect. Throughout her upbringing, she watched her father run his thirty-person firm and knew she'd follow in his footsteps. Garcia spent weekends visiting job sites with him and took solace in sketching throughout her childhood.

Garcia's parents are immigrants—her mother is Italian and her father is Mexican. "They passed along a strong work ethic to me," she says. "They are both successful in their own right, and I was witness to the fact that with hard work and determination, anyone can achieve in this country." After high school, she left her hometown of Santa Barbara, California, and moved to San Francisco in 1988.

Soon after moving there, Garcia received two job offers: one at a tiny architectural firm specializing in custom homes and the other in a large commercial interiors firm. She accepted the latter because—at $7.50 per hour—it paid almost twice as much. She believes that decision defined her entire career path, as the job she accepted was an assistant position in the construction administration department—a path she would follow for many years to come. "I didn't start my career on the boards, as most people do," she says. "It was limiting but also gave me other opportunities."

For two years, Garcia worked days and attended the architectural program at the City College of San Francisco at night. Once she had her general education classes completed, she transferred to the University of Nevada, Las Vegas (UNLV) for architecture. Again, she made a decision out of financial necessity and chose UNLV simply because it was less expensive than any California school's architecture program. She graduated in 1993 during a recession, and returned home to work for her father's firm. "One lesson my father taught me while I worked for him was to finish projects as quickly as possible," she says. "The sooner projects are complete, the sooner new projects come in the door."

A year later, she returned to San Francisco and accepted a job as a receptionist at William Turnbull's office. An ambitious and restless person, Garcia grew impatient at having to work an administrative job and left architecture to oversee the design and construction of cellular phone sites for a project management company. For the next five years, Garcia worked her way up to senior construction manager for Bank of America's California data center buildings, which totaled four million square feet. "I was making great money but yearned to be an architect," she says. "I didn't yet have enough experience under another architect to qualify for the licensing exams, so I took a 50 percent pay cut and returned to an architectural firm."

A seasoned manager, she accepted a project manager position at Gensler, the largest architectural firm in the world at the time, in its Newport Beach office. She was largely assigned to fast-turnaround tenant improvement projects and rollouts for bank branches, which would later become her firm specialty. "In addition to qualifying for the boards, my time at a large firm also gave me the basics to start my own company," says Garcia, who focused on becoming an expert in project management and hired experts in the design and technical roles. "Many architects try to be a jack-of-all-trades and end up being a master of none. It's important to know your strengths and hire people for other key roles."

After she became licensed, Garcia moonlit on two small jobs that were referred by her father. She began having health problems, which made her reconsider her priorities. "My health scare changed my priorities," she says. "I realized I was mortal, life was short, and I needed to pursue my dreams." She started her own firm by contracting with past coworkers to complete her construction drawings. This approach quickly failed, she explains, "Moonlighters simply do not have the time and energy to devote to the time-intensive construction documentation process." She began hiring, and a year into her practice, she had eight full-time employees. Garcia acknowledges consciously learning many legal and contractual concepts through Gensler's in-house attorneys, which made her upstart all the easier.

For the first four years, Garcia lived and breathed architecture, working an average of sixty hours per week. She started her firm with a senior architect partner, who was an expert on the technical side. They structured a six-month trial period, during which he functioned as a consultant. "Thank god we did that, because it didn't work out," she says. "He had no head for business." She hired another senior technical architect and hit the ground running.

Garcia made conscious efforts to market herself and get involved in the community, including acting as a board member of the Orange County chapter of the American Institute of Architects (AIA). She also sent promotional mailers to hundreds of Orange County architecture firms, which resulted in multiple contracts as an outsource consultant. Within a couple of years, she started to get more design projects directly for clients. She says her staff liked doing both large and small projects. Jobs for other firms were large—airports and universities, for example—and offered the opportunity to see complexities they wouldn't normally have seen by working at a small firm. However, they also liked working on smaller in-house projects, which offered more direct design opportunity.

Hungry for work, Garcia initially accepted any type of project, and for several years, she was also doing tedious property assessment reports in order to subsidize her architectural project work and employees' salaries. Ultimately, she determined that the varied small projects resulted in financial loss, so she refocused her energy. She streamlined by employing fewer people and taking only projects she really wanted. For overflow production work, she outsourced to Architectural Resource Consultants, a ten-person firm that she trained in her standards and expectations. This was a profitable formula.

Some basic advice Garcia gives about starting a firm: incorporate or become a LLP immediately, hire a bookkeeper and an administrative assistant on an hourly as-needed basis, obtain professional liability insurance, seek mentorship and retain an attorney specializing in architecture to provide a boilerplate client contract template. She also suggests that new firms have two niches, ideally that run on opposite economic cycles.

Looking back, she recalls, "As a new firm, I was overly eager to land projects, and I accepted some clients who didn't pay their bills. While I had retainers, they weren't large enough, and I didn't stop the work soon enough to break even." On the topic of new business, Garcia believes perception is much more important than most young architects realize. She advises, "Don't be desperate. Let clients want you as much as you want them." While Garcia has carried through on many early lessons, she says, "Being a perfectionist, I have yet to fully embrace this concept, and that is probably why I will never grow a large firm."

To compete with larger and more established firms, Garcia put professional practices into place. "From dressing professionally to answering the phone consistently, we set up processes and procedures to run the firm like a franchise," she says. "Image is important to a client's perception and decision to hire." She also learned to restrain growth so they could handle new work. "If you don't have enough good employees, then find a good firm to whom you can outsource. More employees don't necessarily equal more profit. In fact, more employees can quickly equal bankruptcy." Her rapid hiring resulted in money wasted on furniture, a server, computers, phones, and IT services—all of which was worthless when she downsized.

Garcia is an avid reader of business books and biographies across all sectors. She is goal driven and frequently course corrects her one, five, and ten-year plans—advice she gleaned from her longtime mentor, Thom Cox. She approached several architects she respected to be her mentor. After having informational interviews, she and Cox agreed to monthly check-ins where he could give her advice and feedback. Garcia says he refused any kind of payment and asked only that she pay it forward by mentoring others.

Looking back, she wouldn't change a thing. Although she admits that many business mistakes were made, she learned valuable lessons. Garcia sees having her own firm as the perfect marriage of business and creative challenge. "The company, as a whole, becomes the project," she says. "I put in a lot of hours but it's an incredibly rewarding and satisfying path."

Rooten's Luggage store, Irvine, CA

Santa Barbara Bank & Trust main branch, CA

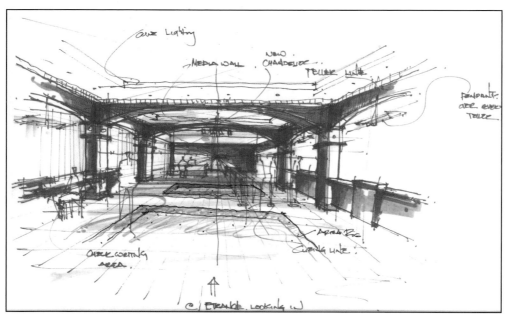

Pacific Capital Bank Wealth Management office

Art Gensler

(Jenn Kennedy)

# ART GENSLER, FAIA, Chairman
# Gensler

The name Gensler is tantamount to architecture. Worldwide, the firm dominates contracts of every type. Built steadily over the last five decades under the careful and strategic guidance of Millard Arthur "Art" Gensler Jr., the firm has grown exponentially to twenty-five hundred employees all over the globe. Friendly and curious about the world, Art Gensler has the markings of a natural-born leader.

Since he was five, Gensler knew he was going to be an architect. While he envisioned himself running a small firm of maybe six employees, he was clear on his career path. He's always thought three-dimensionally and loved building model airplanes as a youth. An only child who was raised in Brooklyn and Long Island, New York, and West Hartford, Connecticut, he still has a hint of the signature Eastern accent. Gensler's father, Millard Gensler Sr., was a ceiling tile salesman in New England, and Art often accompanied him to job sites. Undoubtedly, Art also watched him sell and absorbed the art of persuasion.

Gensler attended Cornell University then entered the Army through the ROTC for his six-month commitment. In his early twenties, he counts meeting architect Henry Hall as an influential force that guided him into a career in architecture. During his twenties, Gensler worked for five companies before going out on his own at age thirty. Two of those years were spent in Jamaica working for British firms. During this time, he says he learned a valuable lesson: There are many ways to solve any problem, so consider multiple methods of attack. From these employers, "I watched how they designed, managed staff, and interacted with clients," he says. "I learned what worked and what did not."

In 1965, Gensler opened his doors with $200 in his pocket. He structured the company like a law firm and tweaked the infrastructure over the years through trial and error. He never borrowed money for the business, even with a fairly aggressive expansion plan, which was driven by clients needing the firm to be in new locations as they expanded.

Gensler is fascinated by business, so he has made it his mission to learn everything he can about both the architecture trade and his clients' industries. He reads voraciously. Currently, he has the following magazines waiting: *Landscape Architecture*, *Interior Design*, *Harvard Business Review*, *Fortune*, *Engineering News-Record*, and *Metropolis*. He says, "Knowing the vocabulary of our clients and understanding what affects their business means we can provide responsive, informed decisions." He believes aesthetics and function are interrelated, and therefore, his staff needs to know the vocabulary of their client's world. Be it transportation, hospitality, retail, or other industries, he says, "Knowing the context for their decisions helps us to become strategic advisors for our clients."

Gensler initially built his empire by focusing on office workplace planning and design. He is widely credited with creating the profession of interior design. "Many architects thought that interiors were beneath them, but I decided early on that I'd do it better than anyone else, and we did," he says. And through these projects, he met successful business leaders and built relationships that he would later parlay into full-service projects—building architecture as well as interior design. Gensler adds, "We started as the interior architect and that led to forty-year relationships and global accounts."

Clearly lacking the ego of many of his black cape contemporaries, Gensler intentionally steered away from the firm having a signature style of design. Rather, he says, "We are focused on solving the client's challenges and influencing design only so far as it supports the goals and culture of the client." He gives an interesting visual to the way they work: "We don't have to prove everything with one project, because there will be more opportunities in the future. We see our client as a rubber band: With each project, we stretch them a bit further and they never reduce to the previous size. Rather, they expand and make more interesting choices as our working relationship grows. We're in this for the long term."

When asked how Gensler, as a firm, is perceived in the industry, he says, "We're fair competition. Our prices are realistic and in line with the industry standard. There isn't one way to do things, and I think we mutually respect our chosen paths. We consistently come in on budget and on schedule. We are known to have integrity and work with both clients and other firms with unwavering professionalism." He also notes that year after year, the company has been voted by members of the industry as one of the most admired firms.

Numerous times throughout our interview, Gensler deflects any credit; he insists the accolades be shared by his management team and every person he employs. "Our firm is no place for egomaniacs or those who want to hog the limelight," he says. "We work as a team, and everyone contributes." He cites mentoring as one of his favorite parts of his job. Many Gensler employees have spent their entire career at the firm, which speaks to the corporate culture. With a nod to his brief military time, Gensler says, "Just like in the Army, there is a right way, a wrong way, and the Gensler way." He's referring to the systems and procedures that run every Gensler office in a uniform way. This enables employees to move seamlessly from one office to another as projects arise, or as they wish to work in different locations.

Through his forty-five years in business, Gensler has withstood several turbulent periods in the economy. After both September 11, 2001, and in the most recent 2008 recession, the firm had to downsize by one thousand people and that he acknowledges how painful that is for a firm that takes pride in its supportive culture. He also points to the firm's "boomerang program," which encourages people to follow their interests and consider returning to the firm later in their careers. Because Gensler has longstanding client relationships, the firm is able to weather the market slowdowns better than most. For example, Gap has been with them since the opening of its second store. Forty years later, Gensler has designed more than four thousand stores worldwide. Other thirty-year-plus partnerships exist with corporate heavyweights across the world.

The firm shares its financial success with all of its employees; an employee stock ownership plan (ESOP) gives every employee an ownership stake. As of September 2010, Gensler's ESOP and retirement plans have some $217 million in assets. The firm continues to have no long-term debt. All of its offices share revenues and resources, so there is an atmosphere of cooperation. Gensler sums it up, "We all rise with the rising tide."

Gensler grew fairly rapidly. He estimates that five years in, the firm already had fifty employees. His first big break was a tenant-interiors project for the Alcoa Building in Pittsburg, Pennsylvania. That led to a referral to Bank of America, and in turn, Cushman and Wakefield. Similarly, he did a job in Houston, Texas, for Pennzoil, which caught the attention of Mobil in New York. Gensler explains that

The Ritz-Carlton and J.W. Marriott hotels at L.A. LIVE, Los Angeles, CA
(Benny Chan)

most of the firm's offices have opened at the request of clients who had work in that market. Over the years, Gensler has completed projects in fifty countries worldwide.

When I call him a marketer, Gensler shakes his head and says, "I don't like that label. I simply try to listen to clients and come up with solutions." He doesn't need to necessarily be cutting edge in his solutions. He says, "I'd rather be second in the pool than first. I have a responsibility to spend my client's money wisely and every project doesn't have to be a 'look at me,' as sometimes that's not appropriate. We do the best job possible and strive to give the user a great experience based on the environment we create."

Gensler is a fellow of the AIA and of the International Interior Design Association (IIDA) and a professional member of the Royal Institute of British Architects. He is a member of Cornell University's College of Architecture, Art & Planning advisory council and a charter member of *Interior Design* magazine's Hall of Fame. Gensler received IIDA's Star Award, as well as Ernst & Young's Lifetime Achievement Award.

While the firm has earned hundreds of awards, including AIA's Architecture Firm Award (its highest honor to a team practice), Gensler reiterates that the recognition is shared equally among all staff. And although he doesn't think awards directly lead to work, he does acknowledge that they do attract top designers. The firm also organizes internal awards, which are juried by industry journalists and deans of architecture schools. These awards breed friendly competition and help create bonds within the company.

Gensler is known for espousing his 80/20 Rule. He explains, "Eighty percent of the work can be done with 20 percent of the cost and effort, and the last 20 percent usually isn't worth the time and cost it takes to complete. So it's best to focus on what really has an impact."

Basically, he doesn't believe in all work and no play. He and his wife of fifty-three years, Drue, take vacations regularly and have raised four sons. He says, "I have a great support system at home, which has made all the difference." At seventy-five years old, he's ready to step out of the daily operations this year. He intends to remain strategically involved, but he has turned over the day-to-day operations to three executive directors: Andy Cohen, Diane Hoskins, and his son, David Gensler. With a leadership that includes 163 principals, they oversee and integrate practices, offices, and design and delivery teams to serve clients in every region of the world.

Gensler doesn't seem the least bit anxious. He believes his staff has a sense of responsibility, and as a result, they both work and play hard while together. "I don't lose sleep," he says. "I have a good team in place and I'm confident in its ability to deliver. I've always made it a point to hire people who are smarter than me. It's time to pass the torch, and we're in very capable hands."

Warburg Pincus, New York, NY
(David Joseph)

Shanghai Tower,
China

JetBlue
terminal at
John F. Kennedy
International
Airport,
Jamaica, NY
(Nic Lehoux)

Craig Hodgetts & HsinMing Fung

(Jenn Kennedy)

# CRAIG HODGETTS, FAIA, Creative Director
# HSINMING FUNG, AIA, Director of Design
# Hodgetts + Fung Design and Architecture

It has been said that anyone successful has not only had failures but also tried several careers along the way. Craig Hodgetts and HsinMing Fung are no exception. They each meandered through various interests before finding architecture—and each other. Today, they run the Los Angeles-based firm Hodgetts + Fung Design and Architecture, best known for groundbreaking works such as the Towell Library at UCLA, the Hollywood Bowl, and the Egyptian Theatre in Los Angeles.

Hodgetts started off as a musician and an automobile designer. He went to the General Motors Institute at Kettering University for engineering and technology, then studied music, art, and theater at Oberlin College & Conservatory. Next, Hodgetts drifted to San Francisco where he studied theater and worked for avant-garde theater company The Actor's Workshop. Looking for a better income, he went to UC Berkeley then Yale University for degrees in architecture. He briefly worked for his mentor, James Stirling, then returned to California Institute of the Arts (CalArts) as dean to cofound its design school. While in New York, he started Studio Works East, and when he moved to California, opened Studio Works West with Robert Mangurian and Peter de Bretteville.

Raised in Vietnam, Fung grew up in a family that worked in the film business. After moving to the United States in 1971, she went to Western College in Oxford, Ohio, where she studied theater and art. She discovered architecture through a history class and found she had an affinity for it. "It was fascinating and natural for me," she says. She pursued her master's degree in architecture from UCLA and for four years worked for Charles Kober & Associates, a L.A.-based, two hundred-person commercial architectural office, doing mostly shopping malls. "Los Angeles was not a significant cultural center—the Museum of Contemporary Art didn't even exist yet," she recalls. "Working in that firm and living in a city that was lackluster in terms of cultural interest, I became disillusioned with the practice of architecture. So I left L.A. and traveled around the world for a year and a half."

Traveling gave Fung some perspective. "My experiences in Europe—Paris in particular—made me realize that L.A. was more open-minded," she says. "So I came back to L.A. and went back to work at that firm." Her path crossed with Hodgetts when her firm invited him to participate as a partner on a competition to design housing for the Olympic Games in Seoul, South Korea. Eventually, they broke off to pursue their own projects, starting with a house remodel. Their partnership officially began in 1984 and focused mostly on set design for motion pictures and television.

Fung considers working for someone else—big or small—to be valuable. "You learn a lot by working in different size offices," she says. "You wear a lot of hats in a small office; however, in a large office, it's more corporate and departmentalized and you learn more professionalism." Wanting to see the full process, she requested to be moved from design to production. "I was very lucky to be able to do that," she says. "There was a big separation between those departments and no one ever moved back and forth. The experience was invaluable."

When their business launched, the Museum of Contemporary Art, Los Angeles (MOCA) just opened and commenced a multiproject relationship with Hodgetts + Fung. First, the duo was asked to design the settings for an avant-garde play the museum sponsored. Next, they were tapped to re-envision Little Tokyo and design an exhibit on the Case Study House program at MOCA. "That was our first significant challenge and was a labor of love," says Hodgetts. "We built two full-size replicas of Case Study Houses, with all the furniture, etcetera. It was the first big exhibit at MOCA."

They approached the project like a film set. "It was a turning point for architecture in L.A. because it introduced mid-century modernism," says Hodgetts. "It tapped into a nonart audience. That was a significant event. It was very popular but not highly publicized."

Fung recalls, "We were interested in looking at the Case Study program not through the lens of an architect, but through the lens of the culture of the time."

Their practice in the 1980s and '90s was an equal balance between architecture and exhibit design. "We liked it because we used exhibit design as a way of experimenting," says Fung. "It's fast and quick. You can build something right away, experiment with materials, lighting, and fabrication methodology." They participated in numerous trade shows and worked with nontraditional lighting designers and airbrush artists.

"It was a crossroads," Hodgetts recalls. "We incorporated a lot of highly creative individuals that you'd normally not collaborate with as an architect. Our mutual interest in theater and film made us think much more as collaborators than typical architects. We saw a lighting designer as a creative partner, not somebody who'd follow our direction."

Fung adds, "At that time in architecture, your consultants were just engineers. But we started a corporation called Harmonica to bring together all the creative minds in other fields as a team. For us, that's a better way to design."

While unique and exciting, their collaboration hit obstacles in the architectural realm because there are many documentation and code issues that their creative partners were not accustomed to following.

Hodgetts and Fung connected romantically after ten years as business partners. Since then, the firm has gone through several incarnations. While the company had grown to twenty people by 2006, they now make a conscious effort to stay small. "We don't enjoy going out to look for work just to have a design department do the work," says Fung. "We wanted to be involved in the project intimately. We're very detail oriented. It would be difficult for us to have five to ten projects going on at the same time, so we keep our staff size at ten to fifteen."

"We enjoy the idea of creating an architectural vocabulary for each project," says Hodgetts. "We don't have a style. This comes from the film industry. Each of our projects is focused on that particular place, occasion, person…. Conversely, if you build a large office, you have to have a style, because the office has to interpret and replicate your design vision. That's not possible in our office. Each project has its own set of design principles."

Having someone run their office has never worked out. While they prefer to design, they found that businesspeople wanted to institute a very corporate model, which doesn't work for them. So instead, they keep their hands in the day-to-day operations of running of the firm. While they see the client as number one, they wouldn't call themselves service oriented. "We don't enforce design decisions," explains Hodgetts. "We're interested in consensus, and we're really flexible."

When asked if they ever take on projects with the sole interest of just making money, Hodgetts says, "Nobody comes to us for that. We did once or twice and we realized that it's corrosive to have someone assigned to a project that isn't design driven. The office culture is important and whoever got assigned to that project would be dissatisfied." In fact, they recognize the need for an internal balance in order to complete the range of projects they pursued. "At one time, we had more exhibit than architectural projects, and we heard from the staff," recalls Fung. "To maintain a good office culture, the people really matter. They have to put their heart in the project."

Both Hodgetts and Fung have taught architecture for twenty years. Fung is the director of the graduate programs and active professor at SCI-Arc. She also served on the National Council on the Arts under President Bill Clinton. In addition to founding the CalArts School of Design, Hodgetts has taught at the University of Pennsylvania, UCLA, and UC San Diego. "It is very much part of our practice to both teach and design, as they inform each other," he says.

Fung says they've had several dream clients over the years. She describes them as "someone who trusts you, who is not intimidated by ideas, and who has a vision." Hodgetts adds, "We're currently working with a Jesuit school, and they're a dream client. They're incredibly open-minded, conceptual, highly ethical, and have community goals."

While they haven't cemented a transition plan, the conversation has come up. Fung acknowledges, "Being married, it's difficult to find a third partner, because there's the fear of being a third wheel." Hodgetts adds, "As a couple, we have to resolve everything. We can't go home and not talk to each other. The business is defined by the fact that we're married."

Reflecting on lessons, Fung offers, "Patience is important. People sometimes don't understand that you have to work and be patient. You don't get famous overnight—that shouldn't be your goal nor do you get to run a building project immediately. You have to learn the nuts and bolts." After years of teaching and practicing, she suggests ambitious architects learn as much as they can before opening an office. "We're still learning, which is a benefit of this profession," she says. "It never gets boring." Adds Hodgett: "It's a life pursuit. Curiosity will sustain you forever."

Menlo-Atherton Performing Arts Center, Atherton, CA (Tom Bonner)

Interior of the Menlo-Atherton Performing Arts Center (Tom Bonner)

The Wild Beast music pavilion, California Institute of the Arts, Valencia, CA (Tom Bonner)

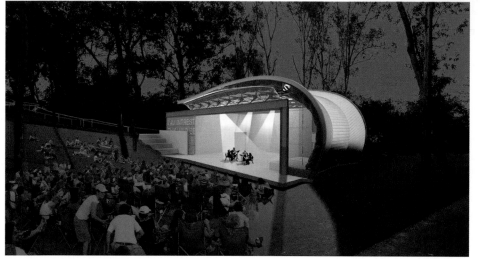

The Wild Beast music pavilion, California Institute of the Arts

Towell Library, UC Los Angeles, CA (Tom Bonner)

Michael Johnson

(Jenn Kennedy)

# MICHAEL JOHNSON, AIA, Design Principal
# Carrier Johnson + Culture

Michael Johnson labels himself an enigma. Until his forties, he only slept an average of three hours per night. He's also managed to grow a successful firm, balance his family life, and stay happily married for thirty-five years. With considerably more energy than most, he's nowhere near slowing down.

After Johnson graduated from Virginia Tech in 1977, he went to work for a small New Jersey residential firm. "It was my introduction to the harsh financial reality of this business," he says. "I made less money starting out in architecture than I did doing summer jobs in construction and selling women's shoes." Because the firm lost contracts, he was laid off after only three months.

Eager to support his family, Johnson called his college fraternity brothers to ask for help in securing a job. One gave him a contact in Wisconsin, which led to a job paying only $8,000 a year, but a desperate Johnson took it and learned all he could. During his year at this sixteen-person architecture and engineering firm, he did both type drawings and surveying. He was exposed to a variety of projects, including Masonic temples, schools, and churches. He also recalls spending his evenings lettering.

Johnson reflects back on his early years and says, "I was very ambitious and confident—to the point of my wife calling me arrogant." He wanted his own company, and so every job became a learning ground to that end. "I would get to a point where I felt like I wasn't learning anymore," he says, "so first I'd ask for more money, and if they said no, I would leave." A lesson he cites from his early years was to treat everyone with respect. He says, "How you treat people on your way up will affect how they treat you on your way down."

Eventually, Johnson moved his family to Georgetown, Washington, DC, for a project designer position at Holly and Graf, a seven-person residential firm. He oversaw the building of six custom homes, high-rise condos, and offices. He left after fourteen months, saying, "It's hard to get away from the personalities in a small firm." Next Johnson moved to Alexandria, Virginia, to work for a sixty-five-person architectural engineering firm. In this very departmentalized structure, he was assigned to production. He lasted eighteen months before taking a position with the Denver, Colorado-based SLP Architects.

It was 1981, and Johnson recalls that Denver was at its crest with the oil boom in full swing. Numerous high-rises were going up and there were incredible opportunities in architecture, landscape, and interiors. Although he had no interior training, he managed the interiors group and was assigned a sleepy project, which turned out to be anything but. What began as a single tenant improvement, turned into sixty-seven individual projects—all of which Johnson managed. As a result, he was promoted to project manager and oversaw eighteen people.

Johnson describes himself as a holistic architect, as he was trained in color and materials. "Most architects are trained to design outside in, versus inside out, and working in interiors was the reverse," he says. During his four years in this fast-paced position, he learned how to motivate, understand, and manage people. He also had significant client interaction.

Reflecting on his ability to manage people well, Johnson attributes his participation in sports and Greek life as an influence. "I was captain of my football and wrestling teams and president of my fraternity," he says. "I'm a natural leader." Grooming himself for success, Johnson also took marketing courses and listened to motivational tapes. "I designed a clear track to have my own business," he says. While he was focusing on marketing, Johnson did only minimal design. He was willing to shelf that passion, as he knew he would return to that role later on.

Once Johnson made associate, he expressed interest in marketing to SLP owner Jerry Seracuse, who responded by taking Johnson on a variety of business trips to teach him the operations of the firm and by becoming a willing mentor to him. Eventually, the firm offered Johnson ownership, but he declined. "The economy was waning, and they had made some poor decisions," he recalls. "I decided this was not the best place for me to lay roots." He recalls learning valuable lessons through the firm's mistakes: "Don't leverage too much and be prepared for a market downturn." Johnson decided once again to move on.

Next, Johnson worked briefly in Colorado Springs for an architect with an autocratic approach, which he quickly realized he did not like. "I felt like I was under someone's thumb and I can't grow that way," he says. After one year, he left the firm and began soul searching. After living through recessions in both New Jersey and Denver, Johnson considered leaving architecture. "Many architects don't know how to run a business, and it was frustrating to witness that repeatedly."

Over the years, Johnson penned architecture-related articles for local papers. In this capacity, he had interacted with Gordon Carrier, whom he greatly respected. After seven attempts to reach Carrier, Johnson simply showed up at his office one day and asked to see him. Johnson asked him for a job, to which Carrier responded by offering his own.

As it turned out, Carrier had been looking for someone to whom he could pass on the Colorado business so he could take a position in the San Diego office. After several rounds of golf with company owner Paul Buss, Johnson was formally hired to run the Colorado Springs office, which he grew from four to eighteen staffers.

Johnson walked into a tight market with concerns about keeping the office afloat. Then he landed a four hundred thousand-square-foot project for Citicorp, thus securing his position and the welfare of the office. Two years in, Johnson was asked to lead operations. At thirty-three years old, he was heading a 120-person firm.

With closer examination, Johnson learned that while the firm had many projects, the finances hadn't been handled well. "The firm was almost bankrupt," he says, "so I agreed to take the position only if I could be an equal partner with the power to right size the office and cut the fat." To that end, he interviewed every person on staff. Some he let go, while others received raises to reset the morale and efficiency. Together, he and Carrier paid off the company's bad debt and rebuilt the firm. The other partners sued Carrier and Johnson to get more payout. After Carrier and Johnson requested an audit, the twenty-two former partners were paid out fifty cents on the dollar over a five-year period. With funds out of their pockets, Carrier and Johnson took 55 and 45 percent ownerships respectively.

Johnson acknowledges he took a large financial risk by buying the firm, but it paid off. The firm was grossing $7 million with 120 employees when he took charge, and they turned it into a $24 million firm with 110 people. "We changed the attitude about design and we sought project diversity to offer stability during dips in the market," he says. They strategically pursued both public and private work, including biotechnology, university, retail, residential, libraries, military, courthouses, and prisons.

To secure work, Carrier spent a lot of time in the San Diego community meeting people, which resulted in the firm winning the San Diego State University sports arena project, a first for them in the sports sector. During his initial four years, Johnson focused on rebuilding the firm, and then eventually took over the public outreach to county, state, and federal projects, while Carrier handled the private sector.

Today, Johnson says their work comes from a combination of reputation, referrals by contractors, and cold calling. A marketer through and through, Johnson still points to their design capabilities as the most important reason for their success. "We didn't elect to sell shoes or stock," he says. "We sell design because we love it." He calls the process a team effort and says, "It's critical that architects don't have so much ego that everything has to be their idea. We are creative conduits for clients, and it's a collaboration."

Focused on becoming a manager, Johnson didn't earn his license until he was forty years old. In the years since, he has taught professional practice at the NewSchool of Architecture + Design in San Diego. "Architects need to continue to educate themselves and stretch," he says. "You can't do the same thing you did twenty years ago. If you see an architect doing multiple buildings that are mediocre and identical, they have basically become a medium-priced prostitute." And when recruiting new employees, Johnson says, "I want to know how they think. They must be able to communicate and innovate. We can teach them how to draw."

With an eye on retirement, Johnson had cut back to working three days a week. In fact, several firms inquired about buying Carrier Johnson, to which the duo chafed because they weren't ready to give up control. At age fifty-six, Johnson is now back to working full-time and knowing they have to rebuild. "When we are ready, we would probably fare better selling to an outside entity, but it will depend on our philosophy and employee's interest at the time." Johnson says it's tough to find people to replace himself. "We are looking for someone energetic and hungry, in their late twenties or early thirties, like we were. It doesn't do any good to sell to someone your age if you want the firm to have longevity."

Johnson says he's blessed with energy and an attitude of balance. "If you're an architect only because it's about making beautiful things, you're already flawed," he says. "And if your identity is dictated only by what you do, you're going to have problems."

Sony Electronics corporate headquarters,
Rancho Bernardo, CA
(Cristian Costea/Costea Photography)

Studio Fifteen, San Diego, CA (Cristian Costea/Costea Photography)

Stephen Kanner

(Jenn Kennedy)

# STEPHEN KANNER, FAIA, President
# Kanner Architects

Stephen Kanner, who passed away in June 2010, was the first architect I interviewed for this book. Liking the concept, he accepted my offer to participate and invited me to his home in Pacific Palisades, California. Tucked in the hills of a sleepy, seemingly all-American city, this home was designed by the modernist as a place where his family could live comfortably.

Kanner was immediately engaging and friendly as he toured me through his home, commenting passionately on his careful choice of materials, the effects of light, and the lifestyle reasons behind the layout. Throughout the space were countless pieces of terrific artwork by his father, daughters, sister, and by Kanner himself. Raised in the hills of Los Angeles, Kanner also inherited creativity from his mother, an interior designer.

Stephen would become the third Kanner to lead the family firm, founded in 1946 by his grandfather, I. Herman Kanner, and led next by his father, Charles "Chuck" Kanner. While Kanner knew he wanted to be an artist from an early age, he was not convinced he'd choose architecture. Spending most of his UC Berkeley days painting, silk screening, and teaching lithography in the art department, he explored the world of fine art and straddled the fence between art and architecture.

After understanding the challenges of attaining financial security as an artist, he chose to pursue architecture but continued to produce art in various forms on the side. His father didn't allow him to join his firm right away, saying he wanted his son to appreciate what he had to offer. Instead, Kanner worked in several U.S. firms, ranging from a small practice that specialized in modern residential housing projects to a Boston firm where he worked on larger projects such as the Baltimore Aquarium. Returning to Los Angeles during the 1980s recession, he worked in a large firm.

Eventually, his father landed a large municipal courthouse project in East Los Angeles and needed help, so Kanner joined in 1981, eventually taking over when his father passed away in 1998. For seventeen years, they worked together on modern projects, which were focused on creating spaces suitable for the southern California weather and lifestyle.

Kanner considered himself a modernist through and through. While he appreciated the charm and necessity of past design, he said with the high-performance materials available today, he couldn't understand repeating historical styles. His colorful, painterly style had been a double-edged sword for him, as his pop art style had, at times, prompted serious architectural critics to pigeonhole his firm. As a result, he shifted his focus to function and was more restrained in his most recent designs.

Kanner acknowledged that his style eliminated 90 percent of potential clients, however he was not about to change course. In fact, he deeply believed and heavily promoted the modernist philosophy through his designs and involvement with the Los Angeles-based Architecture and Design Museum (A+D). Inspired by a museum he saw in Helsinki, Finland, Kanner cofounded the A+D museum in 2001 to promote architecture and design through exhibits, outreach, and education. After inhabiting a series of temporary spaces, the museum opened in April 2010 in a permanent location on Wilshire Boulevard's "Museum Row." A+D features a range of disciplines—from architecture and landscape architecture to fashion and consumer products design.

Kanner calls running an architecture firm Darwinian in that staff gets channeled to the right spot.

"Those who primarily want to make a lot of money as an architect probably aren't doing design to bring it up to the level of an art form," he said. His firm tried to accomplish this goal, but it's incredibly time intensive and expensive. "You draw what you want to draw in great detail, then often either the builder or the client pushes back or changes things."

Kanner estimated there may be fifty architects worldwide who are both wealthy and truly artistic. "Architecture is basically a nonprofit industry if you really care," he said. "Of course there are countless horrible buildings that get knocked out, but if you spend the time, then it costs a lot." He compared architecture to baseball, where players are considered good if they hit three out of ten pitches, while architects must bat ninety-nine out of one hundred—every project has to be done right. However, he learned not to hold on so tightly to his designs. He acknowledged that often when a client or review board gives input, it results in a better end product.

In early 2009, Kanner downsized his Santa Monica office staff from thirty to twenty-five in hopes that business would flow again after the nationwide economic slowdown eases. He attributed his success to his consistent outreach—he networked nightly through events, dinners, and associations. He consciously diversified his practice, building everything from gas stations to low-income housing and educational facilities to counteract the down cycle of individual industries.

When asked about his influences, Kanner cited the Case Study Houses and architecture greats such as Richard Neutra and Charles and Ray Eames, who heavily shaped southern California modernism. He also respected Swiss firm Herzog & de Meuron as well as Italian architect Renzo Piano. He said a project should reflect the spirit and personality of the owner and the DNA of the designer. He also affectionately mentioned his wife, Cynthia, calling her the breadwinner. Clearly a family man, he designated weekends for connecting with his wife and two daughters. Kanner felt that because architecture is such a staff-intensive business, one must empower employees to make the machine run well. He hired bright, young talent and willingly delegated. In hiring, Kanner said, "I seek passion for design, the ability to multitask, and diplomacy in the people I add to my team." After viewing the challenges his father faced in a partnership, he decided to keep his firm a one-man show. While he encouraged feedback from his staff, he said, "I prefer to have veto power at the end of the day, and therefore opted not to take on a partner."

Kanner estimated that 70 percent of his time was spent on design and 30 percent was spent on business-related tasks, however he readily admitted that he was not a business guru, and his staff thought his fees were too low. He explained, "I believe if I do good work and keep my fees where they are, I'll eventually get into that upper jet stream and land the major projects."

Kanner offered a list of actions beyond building great projects to ensure business success. His first and strongest suggestion was to get published. He employed three full-time people to pursue press opportunities, design awards, speaking engagements, and to monitor and contribute to architecture blogs. "The world is not going to just find you," he said, "so you must make your accomplishments known." He considered his Web site his most important marketing tool. He also recommended collaborations with other architects on occasion to present a stronger and unique approach to a potential client.

Kanner Architects has completed more than 150 public and private projects, including municipal courthouses, single-family homes, offices, and schools. He summed it up: "Large or small, I only accept projects that fit the modernist model. I'm clear on what I love and what I can promote."

Malibu 5, CA (Benny Chan/Fotoworks)

United Oil gas station,
Los Angeles, CA
(John Linden)

Ray Kappe

(Jenn Kennedy)

# RAY KAPPE, FAIA, President
## Kappe Architects

Ray Kappe is unusually humble considering the vast contributions he's made to architecture. During our interview, he denied being an academic, meanwhile he founded the now-thriving architecture programs at Cal Poly Pomona and SCI-Arc, the latter of which he started with funds out of his own pocket. He shrugs when I call him successful, and says he just did what seemed logical. This pioneer has undoubtedly impacted several generations of architects and aficionados through his work and his educational pursuits.

Kappe's focus on architecture began during his junior year of high school after reading a book about the trade. His strengths in art, math, and science seemed a perfect combination, however before attending college, he was drafted into the army and spent several years as a surveying instructor for the US Army Corp of Engineers. After World War II, Kappe spent brief stints at both UCLA and USC before settling in at UC Berkeley's architecture program.

During his final year at Berkeley, Kappe worked as a draftsman for Anshen+Allen in San Francisco. He recalls being with a small design-oriented firm as an excellent experience. He worked primarily on Joseph Eichler homes—exploring small, affordable, well-designed, modern structures—as well as Standard Oil stations. "This gave me experience in simple post and beam wood detailing and metal prefab systems," he says. "I thoroughly enjoyed my time with this firm."

"For those of us working during the 1950s, our interest was developing architecture to create a better California lifestyle, and Eichler was wholeheartedly selling just that," Kappe says. "The photos of the homes depicted scenes such as a wife happily gardening, kids playing ball, barbecue parties, and such." Kappe grew up living in apartment buildings and recalls that most people had older houses back then. "Eichler presented a great opportunity to have a whole new generation of young people move into what we thought was a better lifestyle: greenbelt communities."

Kappe and his wife, Shelly, then returned to Los Angeles, where he worked for Pereira & Luckman to gain experience with a large firm. That experience was short-lived because he found the learning process was too slow. He went to work with Carl Maston for the next two years, obtained his architectural license, and opened his own practice in 1953. Kappe gained a great deal of knowledge about architecture and business working for Maston. He says it was the foundation from which he subsequently ran his practice.

Kappe also grew up around business. His parents were in the mercantile industry, and starting at age twelve, he would help his father with the accounting. "I saw how he marked up merchandise and understood how to make a profit," he recalls. "That held me in pretty good stead. I understood that you have to spend less than you take in, which is a simple principle of economics."

Kappe enjoys running his company. He says, "I like the business part. It was never a big deal to me." I inquired if he had a chief financial officer, to which he explains, "I was CFO, CEO, COO—all of it." This same principle held true when he founded SCI-Arc. "Finances were a large part of my responsibility. I wanted to understand the budget and be in control of where the dollars were going.

I always knew how much I had. It's basic—know your expenditures and know what's left. With that money, you can make decisions. I was very comfortable with all those roles."

Early on in his career, Kappe knew he wanted to have his own firm. "I was never a company guy," he says matter-of-factly. He also knew he wanted a small office, citing that he didn't like that the design staff was separated out from the people doing construction documents in the larger firms. "The bosses wander through the office once a week," he says. "I never cared for that type of operation." Instead, he built a small office and explains, "Usually, the principals in small firms—including mine—don't segregate themselves from the staff. The phone is in the middle of the room and you hear quite a bit." His formula has been to have a maximum of five drafters per principal. And while many firms put four or five people on a project in the design phase, he says it's not a necessary money drain. In fact, he says, "Some architects believe an office has to be losing money (on these big teams) to be ultimately successful, but I don't agree." He also mentions that billing, payroll, and monitoring hours is easier to keep track of with five or less employees.

Kappe's first project was for himself. His father put up $6,000 for the land, and he designed, built, and rented out an apartment complex. He remembers meeting people who stopped by to see it, and before long, four or five jobs sprang from it. *Arts & Architecture* published this complex project, along with the first house Kappe built. Later, he won awards on both buildings, which helped garner much attention. During his early career, he also designed projects for several young engineers in the aerospace industry, with one project leading to the next. Kappe says to this day, press and word-of-mouth are his main avenues for landing work. He's never formally marketed himself, yet he's always had enough work. He says, "I didn't feel like I needed to beat the world or grow the biggest firm."

After ten years in practice, Kappe, along with Herb Kahn and Rex Lotery, became involved with AIA's Urban Design Committee. Advocating for people to leave the land in a more natural state, they issued a small book on how to plan in the hillsides to avoid the cut and fill the developers were doing. They completed studies for the Los Angeles County planning and transportation departments, which led to the formation of a planning collaborative. The three men solidified a formal partnership with a focus on urban design and planning.

The partnership worked well for twelve years. Eventually the City of Los Angeles was no longer interested in planning studies. They wanted implementation, which was developer driven, so the work evaporated. Kappe also says, "Postmodernism was becoming prevalent. We weren't interested in making the compromise to design that type of work. And so over a lunch, we decided we weren't having fun anymore and amicably dissolved our partnership. We split the work and went our separate ways." He's been working out of his home office ever since.

During this same time, Kappe was asked to become chairman of the architectural department at Cal Poly Pomona—a golden opportunity to create the program and staff it from scratch. Pulling from experience he had teaching at USC, Kappe built a successful program that promotes a spirit of experimentation.

After differences with the dean at Cal Poly, he decided to leave and start his own school, SCI-Arc. Fifty students and six faculty members from Cal Poly followed him to get started. Another twenty-five students joined from around the country for their first academic year. He found a raw

Rochedale
(Everett Fenton Gedley)

LivingHome Z6 house
(Grant Mudford)

warehouse and fronted the money for the first month of rent to get the school up and running. Tuition carried them from there, and much like his practice, Kappe insisted they stay in the black instead of relying on grants. He says most architectural students learn in an intuitive versus rational or scientific way. He believes quality architecture requires a balance of both rational and intuitive thinking.

Kappe suggests everyone work for a firm for at least a few years. "If you're entrepreneurial, then either look for the smaller firm or the big firm with a unique opportunity for you to take a client," he says. "Most students end up outside the field or in large firms, which can be satisfying, as you get to work on important, big-scale projects. If you're more interested in design, then residential and small work can be done without a huge operation. Follow your own desires and know who you are and what satisfies you."

Kappe laughs at the idea of a dream project. He recounts one seemingly perfect client who was interested in everything he was exploring, including modular construction, energy systems, and kinetics for his fifteen thousand-square-foot house. He designed a gorgeous home, which incorporated both kinetics and sustainable elements. Suddenly the client was bankrupt, and the house was never was built.

Kappe has learned many lessons over the years. He suggests architects insist on a retainer to start a project. He used to ask for just a small amount, but says, "There came a time when clients figured out they could get away with stiffing us on the last $10,000, so I started building in an advance to any job. Many architects have been hurt when working with developers when the economy goes south—they end up going bankrupt. You have to be aware and have contracts in place." He also remembers in the beginning, he was embarrassed to execute a real contract. Eventually he began using the AIA contract. "Handshakes work during the honeymoon," he says, "but they don't work when there is disagreement, so protect yourself."

Kappe has been married to Shelly for more than fifty years and you can still see the chemistry between them. She straightens his shirt and makes him giggle for the photo shoot. "We have always been very close and mutually supportive," he says. "When our three children were growing up, I never worked nights or weekends and was always available for trips and family activities. After our children went off to college, we continued working together developing SCI-Arc into an internationally recognized school." And now, Kappe says he's just enjoying himself. Swimming daily, traveling, and reading are his mainstay. He has certainly earned it.

Living Homes Z6 residence (C.J. Berg)

Hank Koning & Julie Eizenberg

AIA CALIFORNIA FIRM OF T

(Jenn Kennedy)

# HANK KONING, FAIA, Founding Principal
# JULIE EIZENBERG, AIA, Founding Principal
## Koning Eizenberg

"Architecture isn't just for special occasions" is a motto adopted by Hank Koning and Julie Eizenberg, an Australian husband-and-wife team behind Santa Monica-based Koning Eizenberg. The two took very different paths to architecture, but their lifelong collaboration has proven both rewarding and successful.

Koning knew he wanted to be an architect at age three. His father was a builder who routinely brought home plans for projects he was bidding on. At a young age, Koning would enliven them with colored pencils and was eventually enlisted to drafting plans for various projects. He also built houses with his father and brothers during many summers before heading off to architecture school at the University of Melbourne in Australia. During his fourth year there, he worked for an architect, and after graduation, he took a job in a five-person practice for two years designing homes and small commercial buildings.

Conversely, Eizenberg didn't find her calling to architecture nearly as soon. A high school teacher had suggested the profession, and she decided it was a good all-around educational track. By her third year of college, she was hooked and finished strong. Interested in planning and social change, she worked in several large firms after graduation.

They both attended the University of Melbourne, a progressive school at the time. "There was an engineer who got kicked out of the engineering school because he was a communist," Koning recalls with a laugh. "The architecture department took him in." Koning and Eizenberg met during their first year in school and married five years later. They shared a common interest in landscape architecture and environmental conservation.

After graduation, they decided to come to the United States. Because work permits were challenging to secure, they both enrolled in UCLA for master's degrees in architecture and thus were able to stay in the United States. Eizenberg says, "We had two fabulous years at UCLA and fell in love with Los Angeles." Next they set up shop and strategically began to hustle work.

During school, they designed a project that examined the impact of having a subway stop at the original Farmers Market on Third Street and Fairfax Avenue. They met numerous people during this project, which brought them on as volunteers for several months after graduation. Eventually, they were hired—initially for small jobs such as a gateway, a bar, and some additions to the farmers market. These turned into much larger jobs and a client that has been on their roster for twenty-five years.

The two also noticed a need in the affordable housing market. "Other architects didn't see this as a real design opportunity, however it caught our interest," Koning says. "We started to do infill projects and they got a lot of attention." Reflecting back, they met numerous people through the nonprofit sectors. Eizenberg adds, "We were curious and saw anything as a possibility. We did all sorts of stuff, some of it embarrassing."

Five years into having their practice, they consciously decided to have both a philosophy and criteria for the projects they took. These key factors included interesting design opportunity, projects that offered a chance to explore a new type of building, and lastly, financial reward. "That consciousness made a big difference to how our practice developed," Koning says. "We wanted a fit where we could do something of value."

The firm sits comfortably at twenty-five people. "We enjoyed the office energy at that size, however when you're smaller, you have more time to think about things," Koning says. "At times, we've pushed the size to win larger projects."

The couple has a third partner, Brian Lane, who has been the managing principal for the last ten years. He is responsible for staff and quality control, however, they are quick to note that all three of them wear multiple hats of responsibility. "There's a myth that a master person is working alone— like Ayn Rand's Howard Roark character," Eizenberg says. "I've never found design to be like that. We've always talked it through and take ideas from anywhere. You don't put out a quality product without a quality team." She goes on to add, "I think everyone in the architecture community is creative, just in different ways. If you're talking about visual quality, then the way it kind of falls out is: I'm the one who's the concept guardian who makes sure the idea we started with is the idea we get at the end. Hank makes sure that there's pragmatism—how does it get built? Is the idea realizable?—then we may flip roles on one another."

While marketing can be tough work, Eizenberg acknowledges that both she and Koning find casual networking easy. "We're not hard marketers, because we're looking for a good fit," she says. "We don't want to sell it too hard and we don't play golf." They are on various boards and Koning is on the local planning commission.

They have mixed feelings about the value of projects being published. "I recall only one job that resulted from being published," Koning says. "Usually, it's word-of-mouth referrals. Publications, juries, and awards help give you third-party credibility, but we don't necessarily get jobs because of it." Eizenberg adds, "Projects come from relationships built over time. It has always been tricky to determine how much to sell ourselves versus just putting great projects out there and attracting clients with shared values."

They echo the sentiment that measured risk and exploration are necessary and beneficial in building a business. Koning adds, "You have to try things to learn the lessons, instead of just reading about it." In this spirit, they did do a few spec projects that worked out well. He adds, "Looking back, I think we were crazy with the risks we took. Sometimes too much information stops you from doing stuff, so naïveté sometimes leads to great discovery."

When asked about their transition plan, they both give a dismissed shrug. "I enjoy what I do," Eizenberg says. "I don't have a need to leave. The other issue is that the people who have worked for you get long-term value. We do have that stuff in discussion but we haven't worked it out." Koning adds, "We're just babes. It's a late-maturation profession. A few years ago, America's oldest worker was an architect working for someone else."

They have two kids, with the oldest finishing Columbia's graduate school of architecture. "We always had a rule that we couldn't take personal arguments to work and work arguments home," Koning says. "We're good about that. However, we do bring work home and we certainly took the kids to the office."

As for future plans for the business, Eizenberg explains, "We've worked very much at the low-end sector of construction, and it's tiring, as the contractors have less expertise. I want to work with contractors who add to our ability to make things. It means a client has to have a certain budget. The knowledge is happening in the bigger construction companies, and the bigger companies do bigger projects."

The Village, Santa Monica, CA

John Adams Middle School,
Santa Monica, CA
(John Adams Middle School)

Garden of the Grand
Avenue residence,
South Pasadena, CA

Living room of the
Grand Avenue
residence

Dan Meis

(Jenn Kennedy)

# DAN MEIS, FAIA, Senior Principal
# Populous

A Colorado native, Dan Meis dreamed of building from an early age. His college roommate's father was a successful developer who mentored him and introduced him to the working world. He transferred from the University of Colorado at Boulder to the University of Illinois at Chicago and worked throughout his schooling with a local architect named Helmut Jahn. Meis recalls his awe. "At only thirty-eight years old, Jahn was incredibly successful and had graced the cover of *GQ* that year," he says. "It opened my eyes to the idea of architecture in a very high-profile, sexy way. While I had always been told that it's a love profession, through Jahn, I learned that architects could actually make money."

During his three years of employment with Jahn, Meis absorbed everything about Jahn's rapid success in hopes of following in his footsteps. "He was great at showing the value of creativity and how that ultimately translated into a better bottom line for his clients," says Meis. "A lot of architects are not very good at running, managing, or building a business. They don't know how to convince a client of their value. I learned this lesson early."

In the first few years of his career, Meis recalls drawing a lot, but nothing was built. Kansas City, Missouri, lured him as a source of innovation. For the first time, someone had designed a stadium that included a single-purpose baseball field and a single-purpose football field right next to each other. As a result, several firms specializing in sports sprung up and Meis joined one—Ellerbe Becket. His motivation to head down the road of sports buildings was business driven. "These are big public buildings," Meis says. "I knew they would have a significant impact on people, and in a slow economy, they would actually be built."

He had two projects built within the first two years. Next, Meis was sent to Tokyo as the firm's representative for a high-profile competition, which his company won. "That was a big domino," he says, "because I was showing that even though we came out of Kansas City, we could design at a much higher level."

Meis and several coworkers approached Ellerbe Becket unsuccessfully to buy the sports practice. They left the firm and set out to meet with every major firm across the country about starting a new Los Angeles-based group that was entertainment savvy but with much more sports expertise. "It was an interesting because I got to see the books of all these big firms and understand the difference between how someone like Jahn operated versus how a big firm did it," says Meis. "To see some of these firms—where eight to ten partners were controlling seven hundred people and those people were all making seven-figure incomes—was shocking to me. I didn't know there was that kind of money to be made."

After talking to several large firms, they joined the Seattle-based Naramore, Bain, Brady & Johanson (NBBJ). Meis notes that many of the firms couldn't differentiate between him and his partners, nor could they accept his salary. "What made us successful as a trio, and how we really built a practice with NBBJ, was selling design in a different way. The way I communicated design bolted onto the technological knowledge of my two partners."

He goes on to say, "Whenever I go to a client, I have to prove how what we do distinguishes us from someone else, and they can decide whether that's valuable to them. I brought a different level of design and thinking to these buildings, upsetting the other Kansas City firms, which had protected the sports market by convincing the rest of the world that they're very complex buildings, which isn't true. We told clients that any qualified architect could do the technical part, however we understand that these buildings are about event experience and spectacle." Meis had the home court advantage: "Being based in Los Angeles, the home of the entertainment industry is more important in helping you sell a product to fans, partners, investors, and the league. A lightbulb went off within the industry—'Wow, these guys are different!'"

Usually in big firms, a partner or principal sells process, security, and services while keeping designers in the background. Conversely, Meis had a partner, who spent his whole career on stadiums. "He wasn't a designer, so he wasn't going to figure out what it would look like, but he could tell you how it worked," he says. "I told the client how it would feel to go there, how it was going to be different in this stadium than any other stadium in the world, and how that's going to turn into more revenue, higher seat sales, suite sales, and sponsorships."

The third partner was the marketer who spent most of his time communicating. The threesome worked well, and they hired 120 employees in eighteen months. Within two years, they won Staples Center, Safeco Field, Miller Park, and the Cincinnati Bangles' new stadium. It was a perfect storm of the market, as all of the leagues were looking to build new buildings. "We came along with a different story, although we weren't right for everybody. Our clients tended to be private owners," Meis says.

"Usually a city that was funding a baseball park tended to hire Hellmuth, Obata + Kassabaum (HOK) because they were more nuts and bolts and they would talk schedule and budget. We were flashy and selling design. While it was less clear what they were going to get from us, they knew it was going to be expensive, exciting, and generate revenue."

During his nine years with NBBJ, his team won $100 million in projects. It was a turning point, and they asked to be made partners. NBBJ ended up asking one partner to leave, made another a principal, and made Meis a partner. "This structure made our relationship tougher because all of a sudden we weren't equals anymore," says Meis. "I knew I could retire wealthy with them as a partner, but I'd always be their sports guy in L.A. It wasn't a challenge anymore, so I walked away from it."

He goes on to say, "I had built a lot of interesting buildings at a young age, but I didn't feel like I had done real architecture. The Staples Center is a great building that proved to be a huge moneymaker. What it has done to the city is important, but it's not architecture. Architecture is something that makes people think differently from that point forward about that building type. I didn't just want to be commercially successful; I wanted to continue to reinvent the business, because that was exciting. I was always on the fence," he says. "I wasn't so much a designer that I didn't care about making a good living, but I was never so much of a businessperson that I was willing to make a lot of money doing stuff that didn't excite me." After working with a well-known architect/builder for a year in Las Vegas, he decided to return to California and open his own Venice studio.

Meis suggests new architects start by working for a firm, big or small. "They should be in it to learn, not just collect a paycheck or put a drawing set together," he says. "It's amazing how few are interested in where the work comes from." Meis offers three elements to be a successful architect: You have to be passionate about it—the best ones are smart enough to become a doctor, or hedge fund manager, but they choose architecture because they're passionate about it. The second element is you have to be practical—it's not art; no matter what you think about what you're doing, your client has to find value in it. Thirdly, you need a healthy respect for your place in history—your building affects countless people, it could stand there for fifty years.

"A former client who developed the Staples Center was going to develop a NFL stadium in Los Angeles," Meis says. "He gave me the opportunity to look at this project, but we knew that if that project went from design to reality, we'd have to have a big firm behind us. It was a very conscious effort on my part to come up with a firm that was already global and to reverse the formula; so coming to America was new for them. This way, we brought value and expertise in a marketplace they didn't posses. I went home one night and went through the list of the world's biggest firms. There were two I didn't know very well, one was based in Hong Kong, and one was based in London. I e-mailed both of their chairmen, and by morning, I had responses from them. Two days later, I was on a plane to Hong Kong."

He goes on to say, "I wanted to build a practice in Los Angeles and be part of something bigger—to help them evolve. The result is a boutique practice that folds into one of the largest firms in the world, so we have the resource, depth, and reach. In this configuration, we won a huge project in Bahrain, even though we were only a staff of twelve people when we interviewed for it. If we have a bad year, they'll help us. If we have a good year, they'll benefit in proportion to our ownership, so it's a true partnership. This allows me to go anywhere in the world and pursue projects."

Meis doesn't consciously market. His office didn't even have signage. "I'm known in the industry," he says. "I get invited to projects, then I'm laser focused. I'm more a strategist than a networker. And gladly, I don't live off the local market. I'm not a guy that can glad-hand. But when I know a client and project are right for us, I'll obsess about it until I get in front of that person and convince them we're right for the job."

At press time, Meis announced his new position as senior principal for the new office of Populous in Los Angeles, California.

KunMing
Gateway Towers,
China

Los Angeles NFL stadium, CA

@bahrain The Green Room, Sakhir City, Bahrain

@bahrain Exhibition and Convention Center, Sakhir City, Bahrain

David Mourning

(Jenn Kennedy)

# DAVID MOURNING, President and CEO
# IA Interior Architects

David Mourning greeted me warmly in the lobby of his downtown San Francisco office building and personally carried my equipment to his corner office. He brewed tea as we settled in. From the start, I felt soothed by his Midwestern manners and radiating sincerity.

Mourning graduated from the University of Kansas in 1969. To escape the tumult of the times, he landed a job at a five-person architectural firm in the Virgin Islands. "In a small firm, you had to be fast on your feet. You don't get pigeonholed. I would have been drawing stairs or bathroom details in a big firm," says Mourning, who was involved with projects from inception all the way through construction and given a huge amount of responsibility. "It was a diverse practice and I was running sizeable projects—soup to nuts—right out of school. It was a priceless opportunity."

While there, Mourning met and married his wife, Janet, a schoolteacher from Connecticut. After five years, they decided to move back to the United States. They landed in the Bay Area, where Mourning worked for two small firms before learning about a job opportunity at Environmental Planning Research (EPR) through Janet, who worked for Knoll furniture. He was hired to act as the owner's representative on a high-rise project. When their client went out of business, he and his boss decided to pursue work with the Bank of Hawaii. They won that account, and Mourning got a taste for the banking business. Next, he called on Bay Area banks and struck gold with Wells Fargo, which became a major client. Promoted to senior vice president of corporate development, Mourning became responsible for bringing in business. "I found it was always easier to sell other people," he says.

Until this time, Mourning had been a project manager. "In high school, I was a really good basketball player, but then I played that next level of guys that went on to play college level, and I saw my limitations," he explains. "Few are born with true design talent, and I figured out early that I'm a manager, a coach, or an owner. You have to find your spot. You don't want me designing. Let's hire the best and the brightest."

IBM was seeking architects for an on-call contract to service its western region. He won the account and negotiated a two-year unit price contract—with established fees—for specific scopes of services and square footages. It was the first time Mourning had seen this approach, and a lightbulb went on in his head.

He successfully pitched the on-call unit price contract concept to all his clients. He then began approaching New York banks, which needed on-call architects in their various regions. To answer this need, he opened offices in numerous locations. "I remember calling the guy at Merrill Lynch—who had 250 people in his facilities group—tasked with just doing branches," he says. "Whenever they got a request for a new project, it was like putting the project at the end of the train. The on-call contract enabled him to have ten trains hitting the station at once." Many clients had large in-house facilities departments, and EPR became an extension of its staff as that company downsized and outsourced to them. The method shaved sixty to ninety days off a project schedule because the bidding process was eliminated.

Looking back on how he was able to successfully land so many clients, Mourning says, "I called on them and took them to countless lunches." He also did a lot of networking through the National Association of Corporate Real Estate Executives and the International Real Estate Council (which merged into CORNET). "I worked hard to know those people," he says. "It was all about lunches, golfing, and making them your friends." I asked if it's the same today, and Mourning says, "Absolutely. Even more so. However, the chief executive no longer makes the decisions. Now, it's the facilities people or the real estate service consultants."

In 1982, EPR was acquired and morale plummeted. Mourning decided it was time to start his own firm. He decided his firm would only do interiors, and he went so far as to name it IA Interior Architects. "We were the first firm to do that," he remembers. It allowed for a strong brand and one culture. He adds, "There weren't core and shell architects in the company to look down on the interior architects." Mourning also notes that throughout the years, he had witnessed an important trend: interior architecture was less affected than ground-up architecture by downturns in the economy.

In order to build a global company, Mourning structured the on-call accounts to be a significant percentage of his business. Additionally, he opened multiple offices, with the first being in Los Angeles, where he had a strong relationship with IBM and Hughes Aircraft. He then added offices in Orange County, New York, and San Francisco—all within his first year. His clients leased him space and he kept overhead low. "You didn't have to buy everyone computers back then," he explains, "and we were paid as soon as a job was done." He did the bookkeeping himself for the first year; yet at the same time, he felt it was reasonable to take the same sizeable salary he made at EPR.

Although the firm grew quickly, Mourning doesn't confess to having a natural talent for business. When he started the company, he paid $5,000 to an accounting firm to do a business plan for him. He ran consistently ahead of plan with increased billings—and costs—however he soon learned that the faster a company grows, the bigger the cash-flow problem, as the accounting firm neglected to tell him there was a sixty-day lag between when he billed and when he was paid. In order to keep pace with the firm 's growth, he secured a $50,000 line of credit.

Mourning doesn't have much confidence in partnerships, saying, "I've seen too many fail—and the more creative the people, the worse it is." He advises, "If you're going to start a partnership, have a prenuptial agreement, because you will break up, if not in the first generation, then for sure in the second." To protect from infighting and internal dissention, he set up a corporation with two types of stock: voting and nonvoting. Mourning has all the voting shares, allowing him to have less than 50 percent equity while maintaining all the control, yet still allowing employees to share in ownership.

After twenty-five years in the business, Mourning concludes that while a company can grow to any size and do well, twelve to fifteen is the number of people that one manager can effectively oversee. He also quotes eight offices as a reasonable responsibility for a regional manager. He staffs offices of twenty-five to forty employees—considering that size lean enough to run efficiently and robust enough to do the largest jobs in a city. "A successful office isn't necessarily a big office," he says. "Our billings are almost parallel to the Dow. We lag by about a month, but it's absolutely market driven."

Currently, IA has fourteen offices; however, Mourning believes a company with proper systems in place can grow to any size. He has both opened and closed numerous offices during the years,

Bancolombia, Medellin, Columbia (Eric Laignel)

with useful resulting lessons. "You need somebody who is active in the local business community," he says. "I don't care if they go to AIA meetings, but they need to enjoy being with people." And while Mourning is a marketer, he acknowledges, "It's all about design excellence. Gifted designers inherently foster the most financially successful offices. If you don't have that, you're a commodity, and prices just go down with commodities. However, if you have something special, people are willing to pay a premium for it."

On the topic of competitive advantages, Mourning cites, "Europe perceives IA as huge." In reality, IA relies on partnerships with local firms in Europe. "We have a global network in place, which is rare. There are only two or three firms that have that arrangement. Large corporations are continuing to downsize, so in order to accomplish their work, they have to go to a firm that can serve them globally or at least in the United States. That's our advantage."

When asked about the secret to his success, he answers simply: "Humility. I don't consider myself successful. I just don't allow it. The spouting whale gets harpooned." After nearly three decades in business, Mourning has learned, "You can't dwell on the bad stuff. You have to stay positive—and if you worry about going broke, you have no business starting a firm."

Young & Rubicam, San Francisco, CA
(Mathew Millman)

Barton Myers

(Jenn Kennedy)

# BARTON MYERS, FAIA, President
# Barton Myers Associates

Pulling up to Barton Myers's home for our interview, I actually said "Wow!" out loud. It's a stunning, futuristic structure privately tucked away on a secluded Montecito, California, hillside. Through its glass façade, I could hear opera playing and see his wife of fifty years, Vicky, making breakfast in the modern, minimalist kitchen.

Barton and Vicky greeted me warmly, as if I was a guest at a dinner party. Barton spent the next twenty minutes making the perfect cup of espresso and passionately discussing the photographic art on his walls. Vicky settled in next to him for the interview. She interjected here and there, as she's been a passenger for his entire ride.

Barton started the interview by declaring that he and Vicky were special people because they are from Virginia—a state where architecture is valued and rooted in history. He remembers seeing where the Revolutionary War took place and, in his early years, visiting the homes of Thomas Jefferson and Patrick Henry. A career in architecture was an idea he developed at a young age. However, "Virginians struggle with understanding modernism," he says, "so it would have been an impossible place for me to practice."

Raised in a military family, Barton followed suit with an appointment to the United States Naval Academy at age seventeen. "The academy kind of saved me from myself," he says. He graduated and went into the United States Air Force, spending time stationed at West Point and Annapolis. He then spent five years as a fighter pilot. The exactness with which he does almost every action is undoubtedly rooted in this military service. He spent his last three years of service in England, where he made every effort to see the magnificent, centuries-old architecture from the cockpit of his airplane.

Barton was accepted into the graduate architecture program at the University of Pennsylvania (Penn), where he met and eventually worked for renowned architect Louis Kahn for two years. "I did seventy-hour work weeks when Kahn was in town. He was the ultimate workaholic," Barton remembers. "I don't know how he managed all his mistresses, because he worked so hard and he taught. He had this magnetic…" Vicky finished his sentence: "He was absolutely mesmerizing."

Barton recalls the recession that hit shortly after he finished graduate school. A Canadian architectural magazine offered him an editing position, which he seized as a way to get into the field. He remembers Toronto as being an exciting place. "We learned a lot and got started fast," he says. "It would be like a good football player joining the Canadian Football League, getting the experience to play, and then negotiating a deal with the NFL." He briefly worked for another firm before partnering with Jack Diamond—whom he met at Penn—to start their own company in Toronto. During the next seven years together, they focused on urban infill projects and grew the firm to thirty people. They also led political reform efforts that changed Toronto and made it the city it is today.

 Barton then set out alone and built a successful midsize firm. "Many of my employees and students are the best architects in the country now," he brags. He was offered a professorship at UCLA, and he opened a Los Angeles office in 1985. After spending almost twenty years in Canada, he decided to sell his office there to his associates and moved everything to California. He and Vicky never looked back.

Currently in his twenty-fifth year of teaching at UCLA, Barton recounts a saying: "It is the great teacher that is surpassed by his students." But then he adds, "But you don't want that to happen while you're still alive! You want to know you're influencing, but you don't want to get upstaged."

Barton acknowledges architecture is a demanding and time-intensive career. "It's a high-stress field, and you miss a lot of dinners with your family," he says. "But once I got the bug, I was always dedicated, hardworking. I studied hard, played hard, and I always wanted to be a winner. I didn't want to goof off. I'm sure if you interviewed my daughter, she would probably talk about how hard it was for her." Vicky shares her perspective about being married to this dedicated architect, saying, "I figured out a long time ago if you can't beat 'em, join 'em." She has managed the firm's finances for thirty-five years.

Barton keeps a straight face but delivers much of the interview with a playful tone. "I have all the training to be the perfect kind of playboy," he says. "I played tennis and golf. I was a sailor and a pilot!" But he also admits, "There's a lot of social status from being an architect, but it's not the job to take if you want to make a lot of money." When asked if he's a good businessman, Barton says matter-of-factly, "No. I've never been interested in the business side. Thanks to Vicky acting as CFO, we stay alive." He confesses: "I'm not very good at negotiation, because everybody knows you can always get what you want out of me. It's hard for me to balance business and design because I'm most concerned with the building being right." That said, he notes they have solidly stayed in business and remembers, "Kahn couldn't make his payroll and we thought, *Oh God, that's wonderful—what an artist!*"

Barton says Kahn was an architect's architect, holding true to his ideals and focusing only on design, often to the detriment of his appearance. In contrast to Kahn's contemporaries—such as I.M. Pei, with whom Kahn competed for the design of the John F. Kennedy Memorial Plaza—who presented themselves as tailored, coiffed gentlemen, Barton says he's something between the two. He recalls walking into meetings with his senior associates, who all wore Armani suits. He would attend in his casual dress and found that most of the clients related to him. "They'd see my associates as their vice presidents, and they could see me as an equal, a kind of maverick like they were," he recalls. "That marketing strategy seemed to work really well for us." However, he admits to not marketing as much as he should have and says most early projects were won in competitions. That said, he was heavily involved in urban affairs and gained notoriety by heading design committees in Toronto and Hollywood.

Today, Barton's pace has slowed. "I'm now at an age where I just want to do some good buildings," he says. "I'm trying to get my associates to go out and sell our services. If they don't meet people, when I go, it'll die. I'm hoping three associates will take it over. I want to stay on as a consultant, but don't want the responsibility of feeding twenty-five to thirty people."

Barton is already working on his dream projects: a performing arts center in Florida and the modern steel homes that have become his signature. He favors performing arts centers because "It's about making a room in which people and the artists come together, and the architecture enhances that experience," he says. "Today, with the great diversity we have, we need to find things that bring us together."

Barton advises new architects to work for someone for at least three years. He suggests architects choose a firm either geared toward business or design, depending on their own goals. "We put people through school thinking everybody's going to be a designer, and only maybe 15 or 20 percent turn out to be designers. We also teach people to design independently, and you rarely do that in life. You're always working in teams," he says. "So the educational systems we have don't necessarily mirror what's going to happen in life." In fact, according to Barton, quite a few of his students go into set design. Since architects are so sophisticated in three-dimensional drawing, Hollywood loves them.

Barton attributes three characteristics to his success: confidence, enthusiasm, and resilience. He says architects must be intelligent and market themselves. "I found what I wanted to do. I wanted to teach. I wanted to write. I was damn sure I was going to get published," he says. "And if you want to go out quickly on your own, you have to get known fast. I edited a magazine, I was involved in politics, and therefore, I got known for proposing alternatives." Barton sums up his point of view: "Architecture is like a drug. I simply love it. I go into my own world and spend hours working things out, thinking about things."

As we wrap up the interview and prepared for the photo shoot, Barton shows me his favorite books from his vast library while Vicky begins our lunch. "This is our life," he says. "Vineyards, grapes, oranges, landscape, some travel. We read a lot. We walk a lot, stretch, and do yoga every day. We like to eat and listen to music. We have a pretty rich life."

Tempe Center for the Arts, AZ (John Linden)

Dr. Phillips Center for
the Performing Arts,
Orlando, FL
(Craig Mullins)

Tempe Center for the Arts
(Peter Robertson)

9350 Civic Center Drive,
Beverly Hills, CA
(Stephen Lee)

Ed Niles

(Jenn Kennedy)

# ED NILES, FAIA, President
# Edward R. Niles Architect

Ed Niles has assembled the life he wants. Tucked away in a modern home on the Malibu, California, bluffs, he has built a steady and successful business by staying small, lean, and particular about the work he takes.

Niles was raised in a Los Angeles orphanage. He recalls coming across a library book on Frank Lloyd Wright, which peaked his interest in architecture. "I was drawn to all things tactile and interested in anything that moved," he says. "I also remember building model airplanes and boats and loving that process."

Starting at fifteen years old, he worked for contractors and eventually an architect, which solidified his desire to pursue his ambitions. He began the architecture program at USC in 1954, explaining that there were few options in the western United States. Additionally, he was unable to afford living expenses elsewhere, so during his time at USC, the orphanage covered his living expenses in exchange for work. "I was emotionally too young to submerge myself in academia," he says. "I had huge battles with other people there and could not go along with the California modernists around me." It took Niles nine years to get through architecture school.

During school, he worked for A. Quincy Jones, Craig Ellwood, and others who noticed his drawing talent and work ethic. "There was a great schism between those that had money and those that didn't," he says. "The competition was fierce. If you didn't produce, you were gone. Most of these guys didn't work and didn't understand my struggle."

After working for other architects, Niles saw the difficulty in economic survival. "There's a world of capitulating to the masses," he says, "a concept of doing what the client says to feed your family." Upon graduation, he was offered a job at USC, which turned into a stable thirty-two-year teaching career. "There are many talented people out there that don't have the chance to express themselves creatively because they're financially burdened by family or other commitments," Niles acknowledges. "I always worked two or three jobs simultaneously to survive."

Because of all his work experience, Niles was also able to get licensed and open his own firm the same year he graduated. "Never in my life did I assume that I'd work for anybody else," he says. "Architecture is a very personal field. It's not like being a doctor. An architect can create his own work, whereas a doctor cannot." He acknowledges that the series of economics classes he took in college paid handsomely when the business became his own. His firm started with small developments and a house addition, and he grew from there.

Prompted by his good friend Ray Kappe, Niles bought land and began developing when he was about thirty years old. "You must create your own business, your own work," he says. He set aside money to buy property and now owns two lucrative office buildings in Malibu.

Niles takes a matter-of-fact approach to his work. "I don't try to be quirky in my design; I'm driven by science, not by shock," he says. "I'm not here to do what you want, I'm here to explore with you.

Whether the house is built out of steel or glass or mud or bricks, I couldn't care less. I'm not driving some kind of technological process. I'd rather see the process evolve. It's not about what a client needs. In fact, 90 percent of my design is not on paper, it is the emotionally based discussion I have with a client. I find that to be the enrichment that gives me the impetus to be creative. Architects call designing an art, but it's not; it's a subliminal unearthing of millions of connected experiences. Clients can't tell me what to do. I say, 'Let's talk about this project as an emotional thing instead of a list of requirements.' Most clients do not understand three-dimensional form and are not good communicators, so I have to pull the stuff out of them. And I always work with models, as the communication has to be tactile. That's critical at the front end."

Niles has always kept his firm small, usually with one to three other people. "It's not a committee or a community here," he says. "Collaboration on design is a waste of my time. If you're repeating design, then you should have a staff, but I'm not interested in proving myself or defending my decisions to a staff, which happens with a larger firm." He doesn't see the office size as holding him back. In fact, he has successfully managed as many as ten projects at once. Niles considers himself a good businessman. "I learned from the very beginning that there's a separation between the creative act and business," he says. "If somebody owes you money, collect it, because if you don't get paid, you're setting a standard for yourself. And if you have to borrow money to cover your bills, you're dead, because then you will have to produce garbage to pay it back." He offers up a simple equation: "Don't spend more money than you have coming in. Sign a contract, get some money up front, and if you have any sense of distrust, walk away or say, 'When you give me the money, I'll finish the drawings.' Business demands a level of respect that most architects are afraid to enforce."

While Niles's creations have been photographed extensively, he admits to never commissioning the images. In fact, the only marketing he's actively done was building a Web site. "The traditional media process doesn't work very well. There are ten thousand other architects doing that," he says. "I have one book published, and that got me worthwhile interest." However, above and beyond any marketing, Niles insists that over the years, having clients see something being built has resulted in more work than anything else.

Niles believes there is no such animal as a dream client. "Clients are a means to an end," he says. "I don't have dumb clients that just buy off on things. They're much smarter than I am. If they don't understand, they ask. They're willing to say no and to investigate." He does cite one exceptional client from the past: Johnny Carson. "He really immersed himself in the project at every level," Niles says. "He put in an unbelievable sunken tennis court and a 150-foot-long glass gallery to serve as his meeting area. He was there every morning at 7:00 am—ready to work. He'd drive with me to look at marble and really paid attention to detail throughout the process."

Niles doesn't waver in saying how he classifies architects. "Many architects avoid residential projects because they don't like dealing with the whims and wants of homeowners," he says. "They shouldn't be architects then. There's nothing nicer than someone thanking you year after year for his or her home. You don't get that from a guy you did a manufacturing or office building for—they are only concerned about the rents. I think that's why every architect that I respect at least started off in residential, where you're dealing with people. Without that, you're just a bean counter."

Sidley residence

Juan Diego Perez-Vargas

(Jenn Kennedy)

# JUAN DIEGO PEREZ-VARGAS, Principal
# KMD Architects

Moments into meeting Juan Diego Perez-Vargas at the office of Kaplan McLaughlin Diaz—known as KMD Architects—in downtown San Francisco, I felt like I was with an old friend. Born and raised in Mexico, Perez-Vargas has retained the chivalry associated with his Latin heritage. He's both warm and engaging as he tells me the tale of his longstanding career with KMD.

Perez-Vargas developed an interest in architecture by the time he was eight years old. "I was always painting and interested in the arts," he recalls. His grandfather was a builder and had several influential friends, including renowned architect Luis Barragan and Ignacio Diaz Morales, the dean of the local architecture school Escuela de Arquitectura de la Universidad de Guadalajara in Mexico.

Over time, Perez-Vargas came to know Morales, who invited him to spend time at his studio. Perez-Vargas recalls a holistic environment, with painters and sculptors, in which he observed and absorbed everything. He helped around the office for free from the age of eleven until he was fifteen. When he turned sixteen, Morales began paying him a modest amount to do letter drawings. "By the time I was twenty, I felt I was an architect through osmosis," he says. "I was exposed to exceptional talent."

Perez-Vargas began architectural school in Guadalajara at age seventeen. "Escuela de Arquitectura consisted of two modest buildings in the middle of the corn fields," he recalls. "While fifty-two students entered my class, only about twelve graduated." In his fourth year of school, he interned for KMD in the United States. "I had been very sheltered until then," he says. "There was incredible creative energy, and I was blown away by how different the creative process, the teaming, and the discussions were here versus in a traditional Mexican office, which was starkly authoritarian." He describes a culture of debate and stimulating discussion, which he characterizes as an Anglo-Saxon approach to exploring, creating, and criticizing. He adds, "I thought it was terrific."

Perez-Vargas graduated and began a master's program in urban planning at Instituto y de Estudios Superiores de Occidente, which was doing a joint venture with MIT. Halfway through his studies, a severe economic crisis hit Mexico and the program came to a halt. "I was twenty-one," he says. "The economy had collapsed. There weren't any jobs."

A year later, James Diaz, one of the KMD partners whom Perez-Vargas had come to know during his internship, was on vacation in Mexico and called Perez-Vargas out of the blue. Diaz ended up spending the Christmas holiday with Perez-Vargas's family and offered him a job in KMD's San Francisco office. "The following week," he says, "I packed a small suitcase, flew up here, and parked my dream of having my own practice for one year." That one year has turned into twenty-seven years, and Perez-Vargas has never looked back.

Asked how he has stayed satisfied professionally and creatively at one company all this time, Perez-Vargas replies, "KMD is a very supportive environment. Our ambitious employees are encouraged to grow. It feels like I've worked at twenty-five different firms over the years because I reinvent myself repeatedly. My job is always changing." During his tenure, he has worked in southern California, Paris, San Francisco, Shanghai, São Paulo, Guadalajara, and Mexico City.

He acknowledges that KMD is the most established international corporate firm in Mexico, a feat for which he is largely responsible. His willingness to travel gave him numerous opportunities to grow in the organization and see the world. He recounts an important door opening: Through the Urban Land Institute (ULI), an organization that plans research tours and idea exchange programs focusing on leading real estate trends in the United States and the world, he was invited to join a group of trustees to attend a weeklong tour of Brazil in 1995. As Brazil was taking off economically, it proved to be an interesting prospect for KMD expansion. Perez-Vargas spoke at the seminar and three jobs resulted. "It was the perfect alignment of stars," he says.

KMD is an employee-owned corporation with twenty-one partners—and an annually rotating chairman of the board, a position Perez-Vargas has held for two years. He explains how this transition happened: "My one Mexican client, Antonio Gutierrez Cortina, recommended that I make partner so the company would survive in Mexico, a market I knew best. Cortina was willing to advise them on how to do business in Mexico if I was made partner, which gave me a new role and responsibilities within the Mexican subsidiary." Even after twenty-seven years, he admits, "I'm on the young side of learning the business practice. For years, I focused on the design side, then later in life I learned how to market. If you want to design special projects, you have to be able to find them."

Perez-Vargas says the managing partner, Roy Latka, who's still very active, has been a wonderful mentor and coach. "Roy really enjoys sharing his knowledge and coaching all the project managers and directors about items such as financial sustainability, negotiating a line of credit with the bank, and fiscal planning," he says. Learning the business side has helped Perez-Vargas all the way around. "Developer clients want to know that the designer also understands the business terminology, principles, and how to create a valuable proposition for them through good design. They connect with you better," he adds.

This knowledge may account for Perez-Vargas's success. He acknowledges, "There are so many talented people, and I've become more humble as I've aged. My responsibility is to inspire that talent. When you step into a leadership role, it's more about inspiring the creative process than fueling your own ideas and talent." While he was a designer for many years, eventually, he hit his ceiling. "I chose to broaden my skills," he says. "Internationally, KMD was not launching aggressively, and I seized the opportunity."

Perez-Vargas's marketing strategy is also unique and somewhat guerilla. He remembers being invited to help organize a pre-NAFTA two-day seminar by the ULI in 1992. Organizers wanted to invite all the top developers and politicians from all around the world, so he had to find those people and network with them to put together the event. His efforts paid off handsomely with exposure and relationships for the firm.

With the financial market, KMD has fluctuated between 250 and three hundred employees. "Three hundred is the limit where we can have all the partners in a room and where we all know each other," Perez-Vargas says. "It's a good size and one at which the top ten people can lead the firm."

When asked about the firm's policy on opening offices to service local projects worldwide, Perez-Vargas says, "It depends on several factors. If a client wants us to be more rooted and involved, we'll sometimes open an office." They also consider the personality of an office to determine its function. For example, he recalls that they realized early on that the Mexico City office didn't want to be a production office. "The DNA was design driven," he says. "You can only keep good designers for so long if you don't bring in exciting commissions."

Looking to the future, Perez-Vargas says he'd love to do more community-based projects, such as civic centers, cultural centers, museums, and churches. He intends to push the envelope into the few sectors where KMD has yet to go. "I'm still young and have enough years ahead of me to get KMD into those areas," he says. "When I look back twenty years, KMD had not done a single corporate building. We have started winning national headquarter projects for big American companies in Latin America. In the United States, we would not even have made the short list. The international arena allowed us to break into new markets and be more innovative." He explains that the U.S. market is inherently more conservative, so it would be harder for KMD to land projects domestically than abroad. Ironically though, he admits that U.S. companies felt confident hiring them in lesser-known markets because they are an American company.

Undoubtedly, Perez-Vargas's multiculturalism and awareness of the world market has aided his career. "Throughout my career, I have enjoyed analyzing market trends as a source of inspiration," he says. "The combination of creative research and artistic processes gives me a solid foundation for my practice and allows me to energize the collaborative interaction with clients. There is always something new to discover and contribute to society through innovative design and architecture."

Seongnam City Hall, Seoul, Korea

Cinepolis headquarters,
Morelia, Mexico

Public Utilities
Commission headquarters,
San Francisco, CA

*Jie Fang Daily News* headquarters,
Shanghai, China

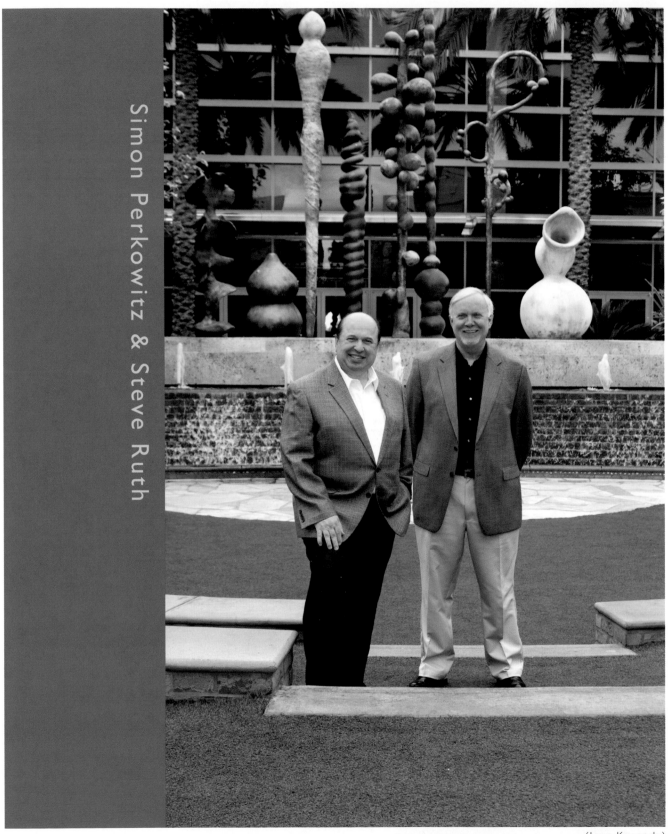

Simon Perkowitz & Steve Ruth

(Jenn Kennedy)

# SIMON PERKOWITZ, AIA, CEO and President
# STEVE RUTH, AIA, Executive Vice President
# Perkowitz+Ruth Architects

Simon Perkowitz and Steve Ruth have settled into a seamless stride. Partners in the firm of Perkowitz+Ruth Architects for more than thirty years, the two finish each other's sentences and laugh easily as they recount their successful rise.

Reflecting back to his beginnings, Perkowitz found architecture somewhat by accident. While attending Los Angeles City College, he took a job running a blueprint machine in an architect's office. Proficient at both math and science, he took drafting courses and eventually transferred into the architecture program at Cal Poly San Luis Obispo. After graduation, he returned to Mackel Associates, where he spent a total of ten years. "Larry Mackel was a valuable mentor," Perkowitz says. "I worked for Larry in my early years when I was still deciding whether I wanted to be an architect. I wasn't even sure while I was in college, but Larry pushed me and I had a lot of respect for him. He was a positive mentor with an encouraging style and approach to business and architecture." Mackel Associates is also where Perkowitz met Ruth and Larry Musil, his original partners. Eventually, the firm transitioned into development work, however they still wanted to pursue traditional architecture, so the three started their own firm in 1979.

Ruth recalls Perkowitz making an impression when he came on to the Mackel Associates in 1974. "Simon was the dynamic leader of the firm and had an entrepreneurial spirit that made an impression on me," Ruth recalls. The firm they worked for began pursuing predominantly development projects, so Ruth, Perkowitz, and Musil split off in 1979 to found their own company, Musil, Perkowitz and Ruth. Perkowitz adds, "We were the impetus for all the work that was coming into that firm, which is why we also decided it was time to go."

They opened their doors with six employees and every intention of staying small. In the original configuration, Perkowitz and Ruth encouraged the design side and ran the operations and business side of the company together, while Musil focused on business development. "We didn't want to manage a big operation," Perkowitz says. "But we were lucky enough to have good clients who encouraged us to grow and wanted to give us work right from the beginning."

The company grew to twelve employees after five years, and then exploded to 160 people after ten years in business. They had six branch offices, all of which focused primarily on retail and commercial work. "Times were good," says Perkowitz, "and we kept growing."

After eighteen years, the partnership with Musil dissolved in 1997. Musil took all the out-of-state offices because he wanted to be a national firm, and Perkowitz and Ruth felt those offices weren't structured the way they wanted. They opted to keep the two California-based offices.

In the years since, Perkowitz and Ruth complement each other in running the company. Perkowitz handles more broad-picture financial and general-policy management and business development, while Ruth runs day-to-day operations and the technical aspects.

Neither of them are design leads. Rather, says Ruth, "We have partners and staff members who are strong designers." Perkowitz adds, "The firm has become well-known for design, however we're fundamentally a service business. We pay attention to detail, respond to client needs quickly, and rise to the occasion—those are important aspects of what we do. That's what makes clients come back."

In light of the recent recession, Ruth says, "We've learned that diversification is important. We've primarily been a retail firm, so we're struggling right now, as is nearly every architectural firm. But the diversification we've created in retail has served us very well historically. We had core repeat clients, and we could afford to take more risks on other projects to allow employees to be creative."

After thirty years in business, Perkowitz says, "We have a good reputation and we've made a mark, so people know who we are." Nevertheless, they employ a marketing staff and actively participate in trade organizations, including the AIA and International Council of Shopping Centers (ICSC), a primary trade organization for their firm's focus. Perkowitz served on various ICSC committees for more than ten years, which he acknowledges indirectly led to business.

Ruth notes that they encourage their project managers to take responsibility for marketing the firm as well. Knowing that clients want to be associated with firms with proven products, he says, "Clients need to feel confident and know you understand their business, which we do. In fact, we're known as a business that practices architecture."

As for factors in their success, Perkowitz says, "We took advantage of the good economic times and maintained relationships with people who wanted to give us more work. We are also fair to our employees, so people see the benefit to working for our firm. In the down years, we had to make adjustments, which I see as an opportunity to restructure correct what wasn't working well." That said, they have largely built their firm as supermarket architects, which he calls a necessity, adding, "Supermarkets survive economic downturns better than other businesses."

Together, they recall several projects that catapulted the firm into a different type of architecture and clientele: Bridgeport Village, a Portland, Oregon-based commercial place-making design project, which won awards, and Bella Terra, an entertainment complex. They also created a division within Perkowitz+Ruth called Studio One Eleven, an integrated practice of architecture and urban design dedicated to creating more vibrant communities. Perkowitz considers these projects their entry into urban planning and inner city redevelopment work.

Perkowitz stresses the need for architects to better understand the business side of the profession. "There are so many aspects to running a business, especially a good-size business—from law to accounting," he says. "Students should take business classes and develop knowledge of how to make a profit." While he acknowledges making a good living, he says that is somewhat rare: "If you have a passion, pursue it. Lawyers, doctors, and accountants tend to make more money; however architecture is an exciting and rewarding career that offers a comfortable salary." Ruth adds, "I agree that passion is key. There are easier ways to make money, but there aren't many that are as fulfilling if you have a love for it."

As for the key indicators of someone who will excel in architecture, Ruth says, "People who do well are problem solvers who have passion and an unending desire to be successful and entrepreneurial. Enthusiasm has to be guided by knowledge." He adds, "People who are young in the profession

Lincoln & Rose, Venice, CA, a project of Studio One Eleven at Perkowitz+Ruth Architects

Blackhawk Plaza, Danville, CA

think they should know everything. Architecture is a field where it's not possible to ever know it all. Senior people only expect younger people to ask questions and be hungry to learn."

Perkowitz thinks a charismatic personality is incredibly important. "Successful architects can get people's attention when they speak, make clients feel confident with humor or a positive outlook, and end up on top of the game," he says. "Integrity also leads to a good rapport and critical trust with clients." As for advice, he says, "To know what you don't know is a great characteristic. You don't always have to have all the answers. Clients don't expect an immediate answer to every question."

Balancing family life has always been challenging for both men. "You have to have a life partner who is willing to be flexible, which I do," says Ruth. "The hours are nine to five but they're not consistent." Perkowitz is divorced and says, "Once you decide to run your own business, you need a spouse who understands and accepts the challenges, or it probably won't survive. Being in a strong leadership position has its drawbacks, which can take a toll on the family."

Perkowitz and Ruth have enjoyed a long-standing, successful partnership and look forward to the transition into a much-deserved retirement. They have started to develop a plan, which includes ownership succession and the selling of stock to fifty key employees, who include both administrative and architectural staff.

Perkowitz sums it up: "Firms don't always know what the future holds once the founding partners retire. We felt it was very important to start addressing this issue to ensure the longevity of our company. We made a decision to actively transfer leadership and ownership to the next generation. Together we want to make sure that the firm will be around for many years to come, regardless of what the future holds for Steve and me."

Jiang Xia CBD,
Wuhan, China

Pacific Theatres Glendale 18 at Americana at Brand, Glendale, CA

Randy Peterson

(Jenn Kennedy)

# RANDY PETERSON, FAIA, President and CEO
# HMC Architects

Taking the helm of an established firm comes with its own set of challenges. Randy Peterson acknowledges that Harish Morgan Causey (HMC) had a complete generational change when he took over as president and CEO in 2004. The company was sixty-four years old at that point and both the management and the systems were running largely on tradition. "We have a lot of great people," he says. "We got together to really question what we wanted to be as a company, and then took steps to change."

Peterson recalls that he made a bet with his fifth grade teacher that he would become an architect. He says, "I was always drawing as a kid and knew that's where I was heading." Raised in Phoenix, Arizona, he took drafting classes in high school then transitioned into the undergraduate program in architecture and engineering at Arizona State University. Peterson transferred to Kansas State University for the professional phase of his architecture degree and names his dean, Bern Forrester, as someone who made an impact on him during his early years.

After graduation, he returned to Phoenix for a yearlong drafting job with Dave Kenyon. During Peterson's early years, he found a mentor in maverick architect Al Beadle. Peterson says, "He was rooted in modernism and became a friend and a guide." They met when Peterson cold called him and said he liked his work. Beadle invited him to come by and view his portfolio. That began a long friendship that encompassed all things architecture and current events.

Eventually, Beadle referred Peterson for a job in Palm Desert, California, as a drafting intern in a small firm doing banks and office buildings. Next he moved to Carli Architecture, a ten-person office in San Diego, for a position as job captain. During his three years there, he did both design and development work such as feasibility studies and site-planning exercises to determine the yield on a project. Peterson then took a design job with Neptune Thomas Davis (NTD) for eight years and worked up to associate in charge of design, specializing in education and elderly care facilities.

Wanting to design at a higher level, Peterson moved to HMC, where he led design for the San Diego office. His team grew from seven to fifty, and he eventually took over the management of the office three years later. Peterson was promoted to main principal for six years, and then became president and CEO of the entire firm. He acknowledges his interpersonal skills as an asset, saying, "My wife says I can talk to anybody. As one of eight kids, I learned early on how to get along and how to work together, which translates to business management."

As for his business approach, he says, "I enter into deals on a handshake and always live up to my end of the agreement." Peterson keeps it simple by saying, "I am open, honest, and direct with people. Some people appreciate it and others see it as confrontational." Peterson also has a philosophy of management: "It's important that the staff does what they love. If you ask them to consistently do something else, they will struggle and give less than 100 percent." People have their own skill sets. Conceding that he's not the most proficient technician, he says, "You have to realize your strength and gravitate to that area. Hopefully your passion and your strength are one and the same, because otherwise a manager has to decide."

Another tough transition for some architects is going from being a peer to managing peers. "An outsider wouldn't have those relationships and wouldn't anguish over decisions," Peterson says, "however, they also wouldn't have the insider understanding of the culture of the firm, so I have to weigh both when thinking about who fits best where."

Historically, HMC—founded in 1940—was known for exceptional service; however with Peterson at the helm, the company decided to pursue a design reputation as well. "That combination leads to success because it's a unique and difficult balance to achieve," Peterson says. "Quality design is visually pleasing and will enhance people's lives. However, if you're only focused on design, you won't be invited back to do more projects. Service matters in equal measure." Prior to Peterson, the firm lacked management structure. Offices were being run in various ways and were managing projects differently. He brought uniform protocol and procedure to all locations.

HMC intentionally forgoes a signature look. Peterson explains, "Our projects are unique to our clients and driven by functionality." He explains that research supports the idea that a well-designed facility—for example, one with more natural light—will enhance learning. HMC and their clients are partnering on research to enhance learning (in the case of schools) and/ or healing (in the case of hospitals). As part of this commitment, he is on the board of the Academy of Neuroscience for Architecture (ANFA), which seeks to better understand how individuals respond to their built environment. Scientists utilize hard science (information that comes directly from brain) as opposed to soft science (interviewing someone) to interpret how subjects respond to various HMC designs. They achieve this by recording brain response in subjects who are placed into a 3-D virtual reality environment that replicates a design. These fly-throughs take a viewer through a virtual cave where the image is projected with dimension and their brain activity is recorded. Such projects have created deep and strategic partnerships for Peterson and HMC with the science and academic communities.

Peterson doesn't believe everyone is cut out to run his or her own practice. "It's hard to do the design work, the construction documents, and supervise construction and staff, all while soliciting new work," he says. "There are so many components to being in business and that is why some of the best firms are partnerships where the heads have different strengths. You don't have to be the renaissance person."

Looking toward the future, Peterson says, "It would be nice to do something new and different. A billion-dollar job would be good for the company bottom line, but some of the most rewarding are the small jobs where you're really in the trenches. I enjoy both healthcare and education projects because these clients have very specific needs and problems to solve." His answer to a dream project combines both: a teaching hospital.

Networking is one of Peterson's daily responsibilities, as is the case for all senior management at HMC. "There are opportunities everywhere," he says. "I attend dinners, fund-raisers, play in golf tournaments, sponsor banquets, and go to conferences in support of our clients." He has also chaired committees for AIA and design competitions for other organizations. "Sometimes projects arise years later, and they choose us because they had a positive experience while working with me on something charity based," he explains.

The Preuss School
at UC San Diego, CA
(Jim Brady)

San Elijo Elementary School, San Marcos, CA (David Fennema/HMC Architecs)

While its specialty is education and healthcare, HMC has also done a range of other projects, including banks, vet clinics, churches, and AAA offices (a referral), which Peterson calls projects of opportunity since they don't spend money or time chasing them down. He sees most new projects coming to them organically as a result of doing good work and having strong relationships, and he considers community involvement with customers as a much more valuable use of time for a regional firm than getting published in editorial outlets. "Our clients pay less attention to published work," he says, "however, drive-bys of current projects are a huge lead to next projects." That said, he acknowledges that "to achieve our ultimate goal of becoming a national firm, we need to commit to more strategic promotion."

Peterson worked very long hours to get where he is today. "I've missed too many family dinners, but my wife helps me find balance," he says. "I don't have a lot of time for myself, as work requires a lot of hours and family gets the rest." Characteristics that Peterson believes make a successful architect include: sensitivity to design, willingness to collaborate versus doing projects alone, and passion for the process. "A team player is key, because no one can convince me that one person alone can create something better than that person working with the input of a team," he says. "People have to love the process and get fulfillment through the journey, because architecture is a huge commitment that's not likely going to make them wealthy." He goes on to say that HMC equally values the three primary areas in architecture: design, technical, management. "We realize that all are equally important to have success," he says. "A firm needs to have a balanced staff if they want to be known as both designers and project managers." But, quoting his father, he says, "When it comes down to it, business is 90 percent common sense."

First People's Hospital, Shunde District, China
(HMC Architects and Shunde Architecture Design Institute)

Michael Patrick Porter

(Jenn Kennedy)

# MICHAEL PATRICK PORTER, AIA, President
## Michael Patrick Porter Architect

I met Michael Patrick Porter at his Santa Barbara hillside home. He and his wife, Lori, collaborated on the design of their modern house to accommodate both their love of art and their active social schedule. An extrovert, Michael sometimes hosts numerous functions at his home in a single weekend.

Michael took a circuitous path to architecture. When he entered college, all architecture programs were at capacity, so he chose an adjacent field at Cal Poly Pomona—city planning. Upon graduation, he worked for the City of San Juan Capistrano, where he ran various projects, including a design competition for a library, where he regularly interacted with architects. A dream he remembers having as far back as the fourth grade, Michael never shook the desire to pursue a career in architecture.

At age thirty, he took a leap and began working for an engineer and an architect, Mark Singer. During this time, he taught himself the information necessary to pass the exams for accreditation. After five years, Michael went out on his own, partnering with others who were design oriented but not licensed.

Michael acknowledges that while he started his architecture career a bit later than most, working in city planning first created an upside in that he understood the presentation and permitting process intimately. This proved an asset in his time working under Singer, where he was enlisted to make all the firm's presentations. Eventually, he was pigeonholed as the political guy and wanted to do other tasks. Today, he acknowledges that all that experience worked to his advantage, as he can push the envelope on regulations and adeptly maneuver that process.

Having a small practice means there is ebb and flow to the business, which he has to be prepared to weather. Currently, he has two employees, which is where he prefers to stay. In the past, he employed up to seven staffers but considers it too much management and overhead. When asked for the breakdown of his time, he estimated it as 70 percent business affairs and 30 percent designing. Between marketing, new-business outreach, problem solving in the office, and managing people, Michael actually spends fairly little time at the boards.

Michael enjoys the people part of architecture—being involved in clients' lives and making a difference. "You're always shaping people's lives," he says. "Each project has a back story, a personal element to it." In fact, he acknowledges that if he likes the person, the money is less important, and because he's so conscious of the process, many of his clients have repeatedly hired him. He tells a story of a family whose house he built ten years ago. The daughter (now in college) recently sent him an e-mail about how she occasionally goes on his Web site to see the images of her house when she's homesick. She remembers him and associates him with her home.

Michael says that while the financial rewards for doing architecture are not great, the social rewards are certainly better. "There is not a social setting where I'm introduced and someone doesn't say, 'I wanted to be an architect,'" he says. "People cite that they couldn't do math or were bad at physics, but it seems to be a career that many dream about but never pursue. As a result, most people look at architects as style and tastemakers. It's something they can't necessarily achieve in their life, so it's assigned a higher social status, which is not related to money."

Most of Michael's work comes by way of social connections and reputation. He networks constantly and notes that work and friends all blend in this industry. Michael considers focus, attention to detail, and knowing how to "maneuver through a cocktail party" as the three best indicators of a successful architect. And while most architects are stubborn, even bull-headed because they are so focused on getting the task done, he insists that to own your own architectural company, you have to be willing to get out there and socialize.

He recently drew a tree to track where his leads and jobs have come from. In the beginning, people came because they knew him—through organizations—as an architect involved in the community. After a while, he was on city boards as well as the Orange County Museum of Art. His wife is also on the board of the Orange County Junior League, which has resulted in relationships and project opportunities.

For years, Michael had an office in a busy area of Newport Beach. It had a large window front, so people could see in as they passed. He designed eye-catching office furniture, and Lori would create unique window dressings, which drew attention. People were intrigued and would stop in. Because the storefront was flanked by a busy coffee shop and one of the best restaurants in Orange County, there was constant foot traffic. This created a great opportunity to interact with people.

When asked about a dream client, Michael says there isn't one. In fact, he recalls the worst client that ever walked in actually said money was no object for a 17,100-square-foot house. His goal was to be the biggest in the neighborhood. He says, "In the end, money was an object, and as often happens in working with wealthy people, they can't make decisions because there are so many options."

Michael simply wants clients with a dream, and he sees his job as linking into their passion. The houses he designs are his until he transfers them—metaphorically. To him, it's a relationship, and he enjoys people who understand that.

Asked if an architect needs a niche, he says that while they are capable of doing many things because they are problem solvers, many times clients don't see it that way. He says, "They want someone who has depth of experience doing the exact same thing. You can crank out the same solution if you keep building the same type structure, however, I believe if you start something new, you see it from a totally fresh perspective."

Michael does take on some work for money to subsidize other passion projects. And he says as part of the process of design, he sometimes sees better solutions midway through a project and spends his own money to make it "perfect." He adds, "It's just how the creative process works sometimes."

I asked him about life lessons he's garnered along the way. He recounted a story from when he worked as a city planner: "The city insisted on a change to the project, so I had to call the architect, Michael Graves, to say the design had to be modified. Graves's response was, 'Don't worry. I'm a really great architect and I have a lot of ideas. This gives me an opportunity to come up with the next great idea.' He learned there are different ways to respond in those situations, which frequently arise in architecture. Graves figured out a way to both appease the client and shine."

In between telling me the history of several pieces of artwork in his living room, Michael mentions that architecture was historically a "gentleman's" profession. He says, "You had to be male, wealthy, and Ivy League educated to enter the field, and while it was a respected profession, it didn't really pay well." He notes this culture of old is holding the profession back and keeping away many talented young people.

Michael enjoys teaching and mentoring others. His favorite architects include Fred Fisher for his subtle, exquisite taste and style, and Carlos Scarpa, a teacher and the classic Howard Roark-type architect.

Michael and his wife are partners on all fronts. She too worked long hours for years, yet they both show up to network for each other. He says, "Everybody needs a wife," and jokes that he couldn't do it without her. Both he and Lori work in other cities and return to their modern house in Santa Barbara for weekends together. They entertain, cook, and collect art—from clients or upcoming talent—for fun. He likes to debate and exchange ideas and believes nobody has a better idea than the next one.

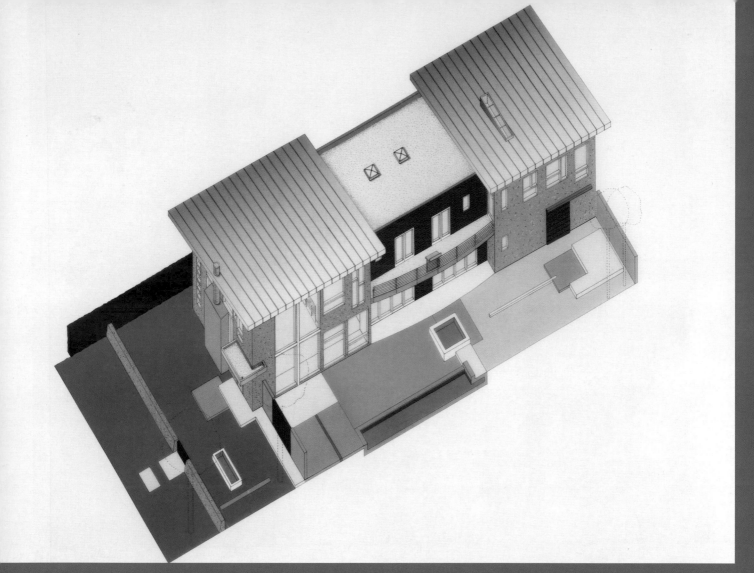

Scacchi/Fluor residence

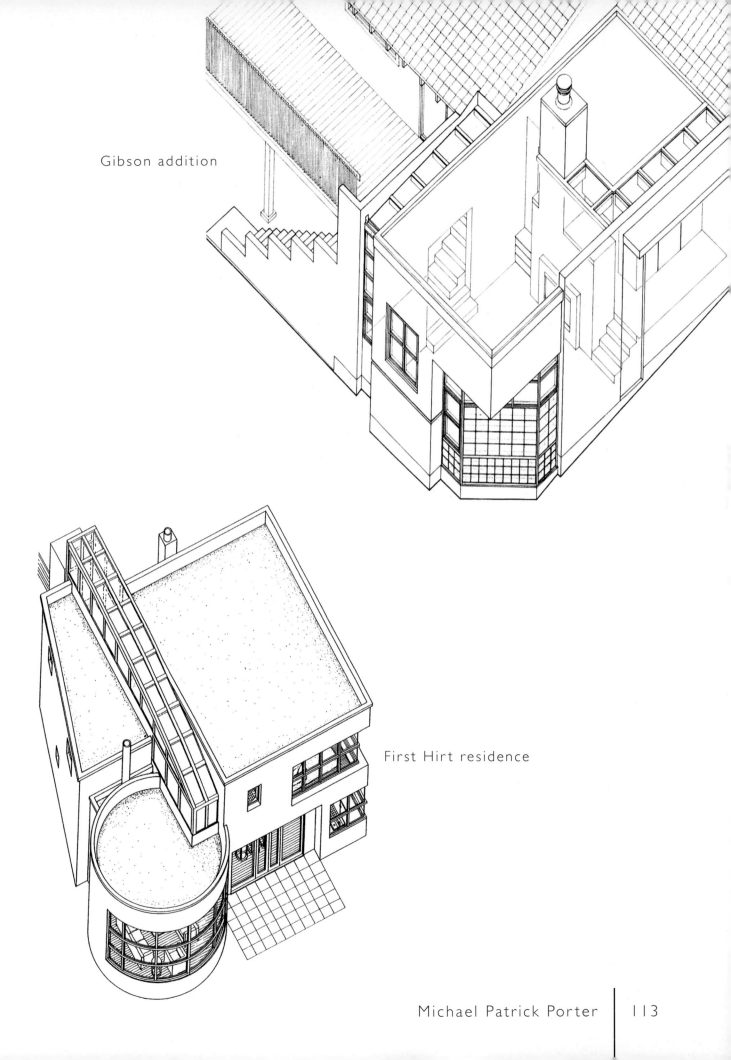

Gibson addition

First Hirt residence

Beverly Prior

(Jenn Kennedy)

# BEVERLY PRIOR, FAIA, Principal
## Beverly Prior Architects

Most of my subjects knew from a young age they wanted to pursue architecture. Builders or engineers introduced them to the craft, but that doesn't ring true for Beverly Prior. "While I did well in school," she says, "it took me a while to decide on architecture." Inspired by a book called *Compact City*, she went to San Francisco State University and majored in urban studies. While there, she remembers learning about Paolo Soleri and his ideas of future cities. She became drawn to the idea of making cities a better place to live. After graduating, she earned a masters degree in architecture from UCLA. For her thesis, she created an urban design solution by devising a plan for a full downtown-L.A. city block with mixed-use buildings and a central park. "My passion was making urban environments better," she says. "I still strive to create a better place for community to happen."

Out of the gates, in 1980, Prior worked for the Daly City Redevelopment Agency as an urban designer tasked with creating a community to serve the families on the MX Missile Base. After three years, she left to work for the Ehrenkrantz Group in San Francisco on various public safety buildings. "I really connected with the client and liked the camaraderie of the projects, which were mission based and operation oriented," she says. "I like looking at the ways things can go together. In an operational facility, you have many layers, which I find interesting."

Eventually, Prior was laid off, so she took advantage of this break to sit for her licensing exams. Next, she worked for Hope Media Group on justice projects, which included correctional facilities. Intrigued by the security parameters as well as the public element, she was drawn to the complexity of such buildings. "I had to create an environment that was good for various sets of people," she says. "In addition to the inmates, the staff had to feel safe, secure, and connected." After three years, the company closed its San Francisco office, however Prior, then just thirty years old, was asked to stay on to lead the design of a mid-rise jail in Riverside.

During this period, Prior attended a seminar called "More Money," which inspired her to switch her employment status to an independent contractor and begin thinking about going out on her own. After launching Beverly Prior Architects in 1986, she capitalized on opportunities for women-owned businesses and says, "I was in the right place at the right time." She built her business with a specialty in justice projects by teaming with other firms on proposals. The mandatory minority or women-owned business contracts gave her an in as a subconsultant with more experienced firms, however, she made sure to have an identifiable piece of each project for which she could take credit.

Throughout the years, Prior sought advice from a brain trust of consultants. A few years in, she brought in marketing strategist Debra Valle to help. Ambitious and organized, Prior was armed with a long list of goals. Valle, however, had other ideas—she said such a list was great for a one hundred-person firm, but at twenty employees, Prior needed to pick two or three areas of focus to build her identity. "If you're trying to be all places at once, you're nowhere," Prior says. "If you concentrate, you start to grow and build momentum." She chose to focus on justice and residential projects, two project types that have different economic cycles.

Next, she created a marketing plan for the residential sector, which included a brochure and attendance at home trade shows. Similarly, for the justice segment, she went to sheriff conferences and networked with decision makers. Eventually, as she gained staff, she couldn't maintain her personal touch expected by residential clients, so she decided to shutter that part of the business.

When Bill Rojas became the new public school superintendent in San Francisco, he doled out thirty different public works projects to thirty local firms. Beverly Prior Architects won a $400,000 remodel of a historic school—the company's first educational project. During the next round of bidding, they acquired another job. Both won awards and gained the firm more publicity.

"We've been very strategic from a marketing perspective," says Prior. The company consistently pursued editorial coverage, leaning toward the outlets their clients read—educational journals instead of architectural industry publications. Additionally, her three-person marketing staff writes articles, brainstorms, and practices her style of guerilla marketing. Prior recalls an innovative plan they devised for a sheriff's conference: In advance, her staff called all attending sheriffs and asked what they liked best and/or would change about their current building. She then took their quotes and photos and plastered them around her exhibit booth. "Everyone wanted to see themselves and their peers," she says. "So we had a lot of traffic, which led to relationships with potential clients."

Prior believes work is ultimately gained through relationship building. "These public clients have to go through a rigorous selection process, but if they are already warmed up to you, it helps immensely," she says. "We always request to meet clients in advance and tour the facility before we submit a proposal." She recalls bidding on a courthouse project for which she requested an advance walkthrough. "The client refused, so we did it on our own," she says. "Once they found out, they insisted all the bidders have the same opportunity, although it was always a public building. I think it showed gumption, and we won the job. It communicated that we really cared and helped us compete against the big companies."

These days, Prior considers herself the visionary of her firm. While she still does project work, her time is best used on the strategic front end with the client. "I was never an architect's architect," she confesses. "I was not the most brilliant technician or designer, but I love both. I consider myself an architect who is a businessperson."

Looking forward, Prior strives to become even better at business. She enjoys creating a culture and environment where people can connect, and states her company mission as "using the power of design to change people's lives." As part of her commitment to business, several years ago she hired a branding coach. Together, they drafted a business plan, coined BHAG (Big Hairy Audacious Goal). "During that exercise," she says, "I realized I had to engage the staff and really get them on board for it to come to fruition."

Knowing her firm had the credibility and capability to design bigger projects, Prior enlisted another consultant to help her get to the next level. That consultant suggested she do an organizational chart and decide whom she needed to hire to move toward that future. As a result, she brought in a high-level designer and business development/marketing director.

Looking back, Prior notes unique challenges at each stage of growth and expansion. For example, when she had only five employees, she was most concerned with making payroll. As a result, she hired the least expensive people, which she now realizes affected the work quality and forced her to be very hands-on. With six to ten people, others began managing projects, and money flowed with larger projects. With fifteen employees, she was getting support with proposals and standardizing internal practices so people could manage projects without her involvement. Currently, she hovers at twenty-five employees and has added market directors so each segment has dedicated focus and expertise.

During profitable years, Prior learned to plow money back into the company to brace for less lucrative years. In preparation for our interview, she also created a list of golden lessons:

- Limit growth and give the company time to adjust to a new size

- Let go of being hands-on with every project and be willing to delegate

- The company's money is not the principal's money

- Paying for quality is worth it

- A company must take risks to grow

- Accentuate the positive and eliminate the negative

- Participate in peer group forums for motivation and ideas

Prior is preparing to take her company to even higher levels with the help of her BHAG. She cites designing a school, community center, or health clinic as the dream projects she'll be pursuing in short order.

Prior struck me as one of the most organized, professional, and energetic people I have ever met. Her charisma is contagious, and her office is filled with hints of her commitment to creating a positive culture such as an in-office yoga schedule and cheery break room. She is married and explains that she met her husband, John, when her career was in full swing. He fully supports her intense work ethic. "We don't compete," she says. "In fact, he actually keeps me balanced, which helps tremendously as I navigate these turbulent waters."

Auburn Justice Center, Placer County, CA (Cesar Rubio)

Woodland
Acorn and
EnCompass
Academy,
Oakland, CA
(Cesar Rubio)

Laney College art building, Oakland, CA (Steve Proehl)

Lauren Rottet & Richard Riveire

(Jenn Kennedy)

# LAUREN ROTTET, FAIA, Founding Principal
# RICHARD RIVEIRE, AIA, Principal
# Rottet Studios

The ding of the elevator signaled my arrival to somewhere special. The downtown Los Angeles offices of Rottet Studios reflect the brand part and parcel. White extended through the space— stark and minimal—and onto anything nonbreathing. A stylish, fit Lauren Rottet welcomed me with southern hospitality.

Partners Richard Riveire and Lauren Rottet seem like old friends. They finish each other's sentences and warmly recount the past twenty-five years they've been in business together. Rottet does most of the talking, but Riveire adds details and opinions throughout our conversation.

Wanting to do genetic research, Rottet started college in pre-med and art. She kept painting buildings and spaces between buildings, and someone suggested she consider architecture. With a general contractor for a father, Riveire practically grew up as an architect, starting with a preoccupation for building blocks. For a while, he wavered between doing exteriors and interiors, enjoying both before finally settling on interiors. "I've found that one complements the other, and I think we are better building architects because we also focus on what will go inside," he says. "And our interiors tend to be better because we focus on volume instead of just flat walls. The two sides inform each other."

Initially, both worked for Skidmore, Owings & Merrill (SOM). Riveire was in the Houston office and Rottet in Chicago. Finding winters unbearably cold, Rottet returned home to the Houston office to work on high-rise buildings for two years. Their paths crossed when they worked on their first interiors project together. Rottet says, "Richard could do everything from draw, to design, to paint." Mirroring the U.S. economy, the market in Texas eventually slowed, causing building to virtually stop. Strategically, in 1982, they transitioned to interiors full-time. After two very successful projects and four years designing interiors, SOM asked Rottet to move to Los Angeles and start their interiors group.

SOM eventually decided to reposition, so Rottet and Riveire broke off with several other partners to start their own firm. They remember the simple offices and modest beginnings as they funded the new venture with their own money. Offering architecture and interiors, the firm grew to seventy people in just four years.

The worldwide firm of Daniel, Mann, Johnson & Mendenhall (DMJM) had been hinting at an acquisition, which seemed fortuitous as the economy was once again wavering. Additionally, the partners saw the opportunities to work abroad as more possible if they were under the umbrella of a larger firm with more muscle (a theory they have since disproved). They sold to DMJM, and Rottet signed a one-year agreement to stay on board. Riveire joined DMJM as well. The company became DMJM Rottet, as she ran their interiors group and built the brand over the next fourteen years. They opened offices in San Francisco, Washington, DC, and Houston.

Rottet returned to Houston to be near family, a move that turned out to be good for the business as well. Riveire explains that architectural interiors are an extremely personal business in that people like to work with locals. Rottet and Riveire have always struggled with how to work in smaller markets, which offer fewer resources. Their solution has been to expand into numerous regional markets, which run on alternating economic cycles, thereby allowing them to move resources where they are needed.

After eight years as DMJM Rottet, the parent company went public. Rottet and Riveire decided it was not the best position for a design practice, so they bought their company in 2008. Now, Rottet Studios boasts offices in Houston, San Francisco, and Los Angeles, with satellites in Phoenix and New York in the works. Even though the U.S. economy is once again in a recession, Rottet says she's still glad they broke away and feels relieved to not be indebted to a shareholder.

During their time at DMJM, a public company, Rottet and Riveire largely worked with American companies abroad. As Chinese companies approached them for projects, they felt pressured to turn them away. "Many quality companies can't necessarily get a Dunn & Bradstreet rating to appease the shareholders, but as a private firm, we can work with whomever," says Rottet. "The world is very small, and if you want to practice good design, you should not just operate in your own backyard." Currently, the duo is working in Asia, Korea, the Middle East, Frankfurt, Milan, Paris, Shanghai, and Singapore, as well as the United States. Owning the company lets them maneuver easily and make different decisions in light of the market. Says Rottet: "We felt we could keep our head low, focus on our clients, and produce good design."

When asked how they market the firm, they say clients largely find out about them through publications or online news. They also get work from clients who have seen their built projects, and they sit on the boards of nonprofit organizations and look for opportunities that are likely to lead to clients of interest. One example is CoreNet Global, an association of real estate professionals. Rottet points out that interiors are uniquely tied into fashion, so they attract some clients who are drawn to them by their exposure in magazines or their parallels to current fashion trends.

Both Rottet and Riveire consider themselves designers more than businesspeople. They have a third partner, David Davis, a managing principal who focuses more on the financial aspects, though Rottet recounts the early days of the business, which included late-night check runs and the business minutia.

Asked if they accept modest-budget projects, they reply simultaneously, "Yes, absolutely." They acknowledge it's both a blessing and curse that they have a reputation for doing the cream of the crop projects, because it's difficult to make money on those projects alone. However, "If people don't care about design and just want the cheapest architect, we are not the right fit," says Rottet. "If they have a decent budget and care about design, then we'll work with them."

A dream Rottet mentions is to design an assisted-living home, as she's recently been visiting several with her mother. She sees their limitations and has a vision about what they could be—if they were more functional and had natural light, they could feel so much more inviting to the occupants.

The project Rottet cites as the one she's most proud of to date is the Paul Hastings law firm because it was a breaking point for her personal design. Rottet is claustrophobic and likes space to feel kinetic, alive. The building was inexpensive but boxed in on all sides, so Rottet used every trick in the book to manipulate the interior environment to feel light and open. Riveire also cites a law firm as his favorite project. He had another client take a lease on space he had previously designed for someone else. While they liked much of what existed, Riveire had to create a new look and feel. "It's challenging to come back and edit yourself, to rethink about why it's beautiful," he says. "We kept what they fell in love with but brought it up-to-date to suit the new client's needs." Rottet advises: "Don't underestimate anybody. Don't assume that because a client has terrible existing space that they won't commit to good design going forward. You have to be intuitive and open. Interview your client when they are interviewing you to see what they really want, and see if you can work well together from both a design and philosophical standpoint."

In Rottet's experience, qualities that make a good architect include being a good listener, well read, and willing to explore. "You have to see the detail of how something is built," she says. "Touch it, feel it, and understand it."

Riveire cites both perseverance and a willingness to change as indicators of success. "Many young people today have been trained on a computer and they think design exists there," he says. "You have to experience space off the Internet. While you can create beautiful images on your computer, it's not true space, not a building or environment. You have to break out of that two-dimensional thing in front of you, think more about the spatial characteristics." Growing up in the digital age, many new architects type and draw on the computer but there aren't a lot doing freehand or model making. When considering prospective employees, Rottet and Riveire want someone who has experience beyond the screen.

Both Rottet and Riveire agree new and aspiring architects should work for a great firm and see as many built designs as possible. Riveire explains that young architects "need to learn the rigor before trying to run their own company" and suggests seeking a well-rounded, practical education in several areas of architecture. "Make sure what you put out there is worth the waste you create, culturally makes people happy, looks good, progresses design, advances history, and has integrity," says Rottet. "Efficiency is good for the environment, it looks good, and it will last forever, so you won't have to tear it down. Cheap multiplexes are so temporary and wasteful. It's important to teach what makes something valuable. Perhaps that will be my mission in retirement—instituting architectural education to the public." Somehow, I doubt she'll ever retire.

Executive office suite, a project of Lauren Rottet while employed at DMJM Rottet, Victoria Harbour, Hong Kong (Wanderplay Studio)

The Surrey Hotel, New York, NY (Eric Laignel)

Don Sandy

(Jenn Kennedy)

# DON SANDY, FAIA, President
# Sandy Babcock

My meeting with Don Sandy took me out to a business complex in Sausalito, California. After years of running a downtown San Francisco firm, Sandy moved his office to the loft of his vintage car warehouse. Gorgeous roadsters are stacked in the lobby, and others, in the process of being built, are on blocks in the back. Sandy not only collected these cars during the past six decades, but has also raced many of them.

Sandy hit the ground running with story after riveting story of his long, successful career. Twisting an unlit cigar in his mouth throughout the interview, he was frank and unguarded, laughing heartily at his own journey. He opened by saying, "I look back on my career and feel blessed. In the beginning, I didn't know what I was doing, and I wondered, *Why did anybody hire me?*" Celebrating his fiftieth year in business, it's evident Sandy answered a calling.

Born in Wisconsin to Scottish immigrants, Sandy concedes he was a poor student. Scarlet fever left him academically challenged, however, he had a gift for drawing. His father put him into an apprenticeship program with a local architect, and he excelled in drafting classes at a vocational school.

In 1952, a friend's parents made him an offer: They would pay his college tuition and give him room and board if he would accompany their son to Florida and care for their orange groves. Sandy explains, "They actually just wanted me to be the stabilizing influence on their wild son." He started at the University of Miami. At the end of the second year, his advisor and the dean told him he was wasting his time in the college's unaccredited architectural engineering program and arranged for his transfer to their alma mater, the University of Illinois, Urbana-Champagne—the largest architectural school in the world—where he finished his last three years.

Out of school, he accepted a job with John Flad & Associates, the largest architectural firm in the state of Wisconsin. During his first real project, the Thiensville Mequon High School, Sandy took the design reigns. Having a vision different than the designer, he rendered the project at night, brought it in, and showed it to his project manager. He recalls saying, "If you had any balls, this is what you'd be doing on that site." Because the previous designs had already been approved, Sandy agreed to do all the schematic design at night so they wouldn't lose any time on the project. The client bought it, and he saw his concept for a campus come to life.

Once the project was finished, he left for California in 1958. Although the United States was in a recession, Sandy found a job rendering, and eight months later passed the boards. After that, he quit his job to start his own company, and shared a space with a structural engineer. "With no wife or kids, I was willing to take risks," he says. "I went through college eating peanut butter and figured, *What's a few more years of doing that?*"

In 1962, he married Carol and started a family. "Somehow," he recalls, "we found money to build a house and raised our kids." Next, he met William Turnbull, who was young and working out of his bedroom, and the two collaborated on a building. Sandy's practice grew with small projects such as carports and family room additions. He says, "I loved housing; it is very personal." In the beginning, he landed clients mostly through friends. "There wasn't a word for networking back then," he continues. "Architects—particularly on the East coast—were proper, pampered, and rich. Marketing was looked down upon. They networked through society. I relied on my friends, and I got published by winning awards."

Soon after starting his office, he began hiring a staff, but nobody wanted to be his partner because Sandy worked eighteen-hour days. "I practically lived in my office," he says, "but eventually good things came both from right timing and a lot of luck." Recounting a fortuitous phone call, Sandy tells of a housing developer who found his name scrolled on the pad at his client's home. He phoned Sandy and asked for a meeting, which led to twenty years of steady work. After their first project won an award, the developer offered him a $2,000-per-month retainer to work for him exclusively in the Sacramento area. Sandy recalls, "That was more money than I thought I'd make in my lifetime."

Sandy states, "I won't work for free. I don't believe in that. Never give away what you do." He tells a story of a client who needed a resort on the island of Cyprus. He liked Sandy's work and narrowed down his search to three final architects. He asked Sandy to fly to Cyprus on his own dime. Sandy refused, and three weeks later, the client said he would split the ticket cost. Sandy again declined and eventually received the full cost of the airfare from the client. Sandy went to the island, drew up the concept, and presented it to the client. When Sandy started rolling up the drawings, the dismayed client asked, "Where are you going with those?" Sandy replied, "These are my drawings, and I don't work for free. I need a check and a signed contract." The client agreed to both, and he won the lucrative project.

Sandy didn't join the AIA for the first ten years of his career. "I didn't have the time, the money, or the interest," he says. "But people didn't recognize me as an architect if I didn't have AIA after my name, so I eventually became a member." Several years later, the editor of the influential *Architectural Record* put Sandy's name up for fellowship in the AIA, which led to a flood of work.

After eleven years in business, Sandy still had only nine staffers and was averaging four hours of sleep per night. After hearing his woes over lunch, a lighting salesman suggested Sandy meet Jim Babcock, a fellow University of Illinois alum. A year later, they partnered and formed Sandy Babcock Architects. "Jim was probably ten times better in business than I was," Sandy admits, "but I was the rainmaker." They grew to one hundred people at one point, and then a recession forced them to downsize to fifty. "Every ten years or so, there's a recession," says Sandy. "It's a cleansing of the deadwood." He considers thirty-five to forty people as a manageable, comfortably sized office where mentoring and creativity can flourish.

During a 1970s recession, they brought everyone together and said, "Jim and I have cut our pay in half, and you have a decision to make: We need to either let eight people go or cut everyone's salary by 25 percent." The staff chose to cut their salaries, and within eighteen months, was paid back for what they had given up. Sandy says they used this strategy multiple times to weather hard economic times.

After thirty years together, Sandy bought out Babcock during a recession and continued to run the firm alone. Eventually, Sandy decided to step out altogether as well. He says, "I wanted to get back to what I love doing: flying to a job site, spending a week drawing, and heading home with a check in hand." Craving that simplicity, one Sunday morning, he left the office and never went back. He presented the company heads with a contract, which included a five-year buyout, a two-year non-compete, and a sell off of his 70 percent stock holding. Under the contract, Sandy worked two years in the office on a full salary, and then worked for three years on an hourly rate. However, before he would sign the contract, he insisted on finding his own replacement. "I had a lot of money coming to me during the next five years," he says, "so I wanted somebody that could step up to the table."

Through a headhunter, he looked for junior partners at firms that had senior partners who were not much older than they were. He reasoned that these people would have less leverage and be more eager to step into the leadership role. In the end, Sandy interviewed sixteen candidates over breakfast meetings. "One morning," he says, "this guy enters the restaurant with all the confidence in the world. He looks around and picks me out. I said, 'You have the job.'" With a capable successor in place, Sandy signed his walking papers.

Sandy describes their firm as a democratic dictatorship. "We listened to everybody," he says, "then we made the final decision." He calls his management style bottom-line focused. He believes in giving people room to do their job. And in an effort to foster a strong working environment, they gave employees perks, which was unheard of thirty years ago. Examples included alternating Fridays off, employee profit sharing, pension plans, and a 401(k). "It's a business," he says, "but it's more like a family; you rely on those people." As company policy, they never put individuals' names on awards, as they saw everyone on the team as important.

Today, Sandy is back to doing what he enjoys: "The site plan, design, interiors, landscape…," he says. "It's the total package or nothing at all." And he draws everything freehand, saying, "My projects begin with a charrette. And I can sell my wares as well as anybody if I go out with a small bag of tricks. I have the confidence to romance them into hiring me because I'll draw in front of them, and that is magic."

Dubai condominiums

Town center,
New Cairo,
Egypt

Pete's Harbor, Redwood City, CA

Rob Steinberg

(Jenn Kennedy)

# ROB STEINBERG, FAIA, President
# Steinberg Architects

A third-generation architect, Rob Steinberg tried to pursue something else as a youth. An avid storyteller, he started a motion picture company doing documentary films for Governor Jimmy Carter after undergraduate school. While living in Hollywood, he directed several films and produced some television shows before returning to UC Berkeley's graduate school for architecture.

Steinberg grew up in a contemporary house in Silicon Valley, California. "I was very attuned to architecture early on," he says. "It wasn't just a profession but a way of life, something I felt in my bones through my father and grandfather's work." After graduating from Berkeley in 1977, he went to work for his father, Goodwin Steinberg, who owned an established San Jose architecture firm. "I was able to get opportunities quickly," he says, "but the drawback was being in San Jose, which was not an architectural mecca." Rob and his father differed on many fronts. His father's dream was to be a local, community-based architect and he gravitated toward an earthy, natural indoor/outdoor style—a vocabulary that did not interest Rob. However, while they didn't agree stylistically, their core principles were aligned, so Rob stayed.

Steinberg witnessed his father running all operations and generating all design. He observed his high stress level and questioned his father's business model. "We went through a painful transition with my father's ex partners, because they stayed too long and wanted a lot of money," he says. "I realized I wanted to do a transition in a slow, methodical way, when I was still contributing a lot. I made a big effort to find younger partners that had great training but didn't have the opportunity at their existing firms, and I was willing to offer them a growth plan."

His father has since retired and Steinberg has been president of the firm for the last twenty years. He has seven partners, including Ernie Amani, who has been partner for thirty years and is strong in project management, finance, and construction. "We work together incredibly well and it has resulted in our business expanding," says Steinberg. "I focused on making every job award winning—something that would attract new clients."

He acknowledges that in the beginning, they took any job that came in and viewed them as an opportunity. Steinberg makes it a habit of pushing clients creatively to the point of discomfort. "It's a fine line between getting fired and taking the client farther than they thought possible," he says. "It's my MO to understand clients and gauge their capacity." In this pursuit, Steinberg has made mistakes and even lost clients, but overall, it has resulted in better relationships and projects.

Steinberg sees every job as an opportunity that could lead to another project. For example, he was hired to design a temporary building, which led to a major college campus project in southern California. He says, "Through working in southern California, we have grown an office of about sixty people, which gives us a presence for future work in that market. Similarly, we opened offices in San Francisco and then in Shanghai to service projects and now we have staffing and reach locally." While it was never his goal to grow a large firm, he is open to the opportunities that present themselves out of quality projects.

At one point, the financial operations almost sunk the practice. "We went through a time when we had bookkeepers that weren't doing their jobs, and that flared into a major crisis," he recalls. "After that, I realized that this is a business and not just about the art. I wanted to make a good living and benefit from my hard work. I want to design and to be with clients." In the years since, he has surrounded himself with people who are strong at things he doesn't want to do. "I'm aware of the numbers and core business elements at a conceptual level," he explains. "However, we have consultants and people in-house who are much smarter in those areas to oversee the day-to-day operations. I understand the principles of it, and I can tell you what a fee should be—plus or minus 10 percent— based on experience and instinct. That's been my strategy: to hand off things that I don't enjoy."

Steinberg points to the quality of his work as the number one source of additional work. People see his buildings and hire him for projects. He also actively pursues getting published in trade publications. Never one to shy away from promotion and marketing, he says, "If you have a good product, it's not hard to sell. People can sense whether you believe in your project or not. I'm passionate about what I do, so I enjoy telling people about those stories. I like to take people on a journey, on an experience of their environment. Architecture is a three-dimensional way of telling a story. It's very similar to the storytelling you share in film. You think about any great filmmaker; they showed contrast, just like Frank Lloyd Wright."

Since taking over the firm, Steinberg has grown it from twelve to as large as 150 people, although they are currently at 110. "That wasn't conscious," he says. "Our growth was about what worked and opportunities we wanted to pursue. I wasn't interested in doing some things, so I wanted to find talented people who complemented my skills." His approach is largely one of collaboration. "Even though it might be a slower process, collaborating with different people gives better answers than I could come up with on my own," he says. "I've set up a company of smart people who are going to be able to express themselves and work as a team. That takes a certain temperament, so it's not a good fit for everybody."

While Steinberg has the final say, he rarely flexes that muscle. "In the last twenty years, you could count on one hand the times I've made a unilateral decision," he says. "We have a phrase in the office: 'Best idea wins.' It doesn't matter where the idea comes from, it's the quality of the idea." He also acknowledges choosing partners with shared goals and values. "With delegation, things turn out differently than if I did it, but that's okay," he says. "It's allowed people to advance and has freed me up to do new things."

Steinberg has four offices, which "have opened for different reasons," he says. "Los Angeles opened because we had work there and thought we could better serve those clients by being there, and to diversify from our northern California office; San Francisco because we found a talented designer and partner who did complementary work to what we did; Shanghai because a client brought us. The office in San Jose is heavier on the developer side. L.A. is heavier on the educational side. So that's helped. All the developers have stopped. We've supplemented with overseas work."

As for future dream projects, Steinberg plans to apply his experience of urban mixed-used housing on a bigger scale. He loves senior housing projects, as the various services needed such as food, fitness, health, and culture offer a litany of design opportunities. He acknowledges that unlike most, his firm can do all of the pieces of a large community project.

Wuhan
master plan,
China

Santa Monica
College, CA

Currently, Steinberg is intrigued with China. "Two of the biggest building types in Asia are education and housing; we have strength and experience in both," he says. "I'm spending at least a quarter of my time there. I think they're going through a revolution in their architecture and real estate development. They're exhausting themselves by doing taller buildings, round buildings, triangular buildings. They've only considered what looks good. They're really hungry for rational thought and ideas."

Through his transition plan, Steinberg expects to retire comfortably and receive fair value from his company. As part of this next phase, his role is changing. "I'm picking the projects I do," he says. "I'm enjoying setting direction, opening new markets, speaking, and serving on boards. That's fun for me, because I'm meeting the kind of people who are opening new doors. That's another level of creativity, of designing."

Steinberg's advice for architects looking to start their own firm: Have a strong vision and a consistent message. "You have to decide what drives you," he says. "A long time ago, we decided it's design and relationships, while other firms do service models. But you have to dig deep, see who you are, and know what you really believe in. Then what you do will endure."

Santa Monica College student services center

Erik Sueberkrop

(Jenn Kennedy)

# ERIK SUEBERKROP, FAIA, Chairman
# STUDIOS Architecture

Erik Sueberkrop is a shy yet intense man. His chooses his words carefully and uses them frugally. Strong in both art and math, he started working in an architectural firm at sixteen years old, at the suggestion of his father, a sculptor.

After graduating from the University of Cincinnati, Sueberkrop worked as a designer for some well-known medium-size firms. His clear goal was always design, although he possessed a wide skill base. "I could put together a set of drawings when I was twenty-four," he says. "However, I wanted as much varied experience as possible." At twenty-seven years old, he made partner—which offered him exposure to the entire architectural process—at Woollen, Molzan and Partners, one of the most well-known firms in Indiana. He stayed for ten years.

The firm had a holistic approach, where each of the five principals was responsible for getting a project out. Starting as the junior partner during a recession, Sueberkrop volunteered to be the marketing expert, something he had to learn fast. Eventually, he started to crave a more cosmopolitan area and left the firm for a staff job in San Francisco. "A lot of people would say moving was stupid because I was a partner in Indiana and now I was just a regular staff person," he says. "But I wanted a lifestyle change."

Sueberkrop joined Environmental Planning and Research (EPR) as a designer in 1980. Candill Rowlett Scott (CRS), the largest firm in the United States at the time, acquired EPR in 1984 and created a new culture and configuration that didn't appeal to Sueberkrop. He and two colleagues took their savings and started their own firm in 1985. Two others joined them within the first year. "Starting a business is about the broad perspective, not the details," he says. "Some people get into the detail and others delegate that. Numbers are not my strength, so we hired a strong accounting person."

They chose the name STUDIOS because after working in a large office, they were interested in setting up teams around a client. "Twenty-five years ago, most firms were organized horizontally, where there was a design department and a production department," he says. "We chose to organize vertically, so that the leader of a studio, or team, is active in the design. Partners are expected to cause design to happen with a team. Sueberkrop explains that this intentionally renaissance approach is a conscious structure to help STUDIOS stay nimble.

The founding partners were all equals. "Our decision-making process is fairly consensus based," he explains. "It's slower and more laborious, but you get more buy in and it's more holistic." It's also structured so that over time, different people own different percentages of the company.

Sueberkrop and his partners also agreed that they didn't want their company to be as large as the firm from which they came. Rather, they envisioned a middle-size firm, between thirty and one hundred employees—which he considers small enough to be familial but large enough to take on big projects. They had no clients initially, but luckily, the partners brought diverse portfolios and contacts, and projects came through referrals by friends. Their first big client was Apple, which needed them both for U.S. and European projects.

Knowing offices on both coasts would strategically extend their reach, they added a Washington, DC, office six months later. Three years after opening the San Francisco firm, they added a London office, followed by a Paris location—which Sueberkrop managed—the following year. They began partnering worldwide with production-oriented firms that functioned as the construction administration architect.

The London office, which grew to twenty-five, didn't ultimately succeed, which Sueberkrop attributes to lack of on-site leadership and the failure of the company to really set local roots. Meanwhile, the Paris office flourished with a good client base, reputation, and leadership. Sueberkrop recalls that almost every project handled in the Paris office was published during the first year. They also saw one project lead to the next. "We are the only American firm in Paris, while there are eighty American firms in England," he notes. "It has to do with the business models in each of those places as well as the firm focus."

Sueberkrop learned immensely from their high-tech clients. "The tech industry was a model for the pace, the innovation, and the dedication needed to succeed," he says. "Most high-tech firms went through some matriculation. We gleaned that you have to gauge yourself as you grow."

When asked if he attributes his success to good design or good business, Sueberkrop says, "Good design *is* good business." He believes that as an architect, you have to be a strong businessman, a quality designer, and a savvy practitioner—the three-legged stool. "We've been successful at design and we also had some luck," he says. "We were there when Silicon Valley was taking off and there to innovate when innovation was valued." Sueberkrop and his partners took calculated risks and talked a lot internally about their vision. He also notes, "Integrity and relationships are really important, not only with clients, but with colleagues. We have shared values and a vision and made communication a priority."

Sueberkrop's approach to hiring is practical. "We don't just put someone in charge, we tend to grow them," he says. "I look for people who are achievers, that have the potential to be partners." And when it comes to choosing someone who will fit in versus someone with incredible talent, he says, "To me, capability is more important than getting along all the time, so I tend to hire people I think can replace me later on."

As for projects, Sueberkrop insists on being selective. He believes that clients and architects have a way of selecting each other. And while they occasionally take on less lucrative projects if they are building experience in a new market sector, he says, "You don't stay in business unless you make money."

While many architects develop business based on relationships, Sueberkrop says most his work has come through reputation. "Our platform is more about skills, capabilities, and innovation," he says. "It's not so much about who we know."

Currently, the firm has sixteen partners and they each handle the pursuit of new business differently. "We don't tell our people to get involved in organizations just to hustle business," he says. "It has to be about passion. It'll fall flat if you don't have that behind you."

Sueberkrop and the senior partners have always had a transition plan in place. "We're trying to encourage younger and newer partners in the firm," he says. And while he acknowledges that negotiating his family and work life has always been hard, he is now more balanced. That said, he adds, "I don't know if I can honestly advise somebody to only work six hours a day. If you're passionate about developing a firm, you'll make the time for it, and your personal infrastructure will adjust."

University of Cincinnati
CARE/Crawley Building, OH

University of Cincinnati atrium, OH

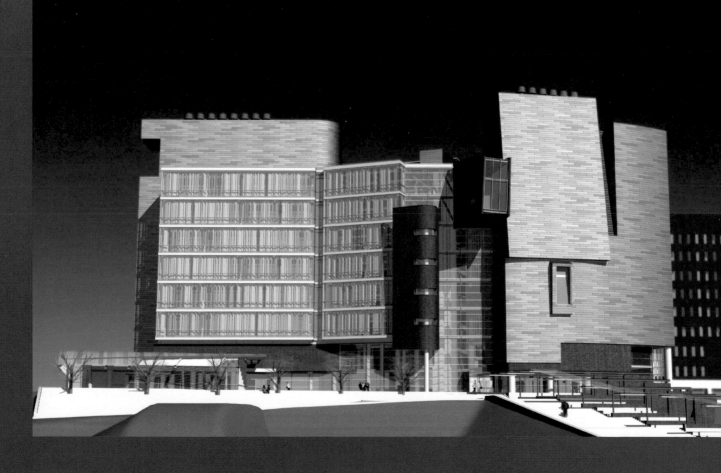

Allison Williams

(Jenn Kennedy)

# ALLISON WILLIAMS, FAIA, Principal
# Perkins + Will

Allison Williams commands your attention. Upon introduction, it's apparent that she has ideas about everything. Modern and precise, she moves between directing and partnering in the design of our interview and photo shoot.

A California child of the 1960s, Williams earned both an undergraduate degree in art and her master's in architecture from UC Berkeley, which was a very charged place to be at the time. She remembers the spark of the Black Panthers efforts and says, "You needed to know who you were, as it was a really easy time to get lost." Furthermore, her father, who held a degree in engineering and urban planning, was very design oriented, and she remembers him watercoloring regularly, and he taught her to draw and notice the use of color, texture, and daylight in a space.

Williams started her career in 1976 at San Francisco's McCue Boone Tomsick, where she worked for four years. She was identified early on as someone who had design talent, but she actively sought technical development as well. As soon as she qualified, Williams sat for the licensing exam and passed it.

Next, she worked at a large firm, Skidmore, Owings & Merrill (SOM), which tracked everyone into one of three disciplines: technical, design, or management. Referred to as the three-legged stool, she believes all parts are necessary to run a successful project. She remembers wanting to touch on all areas, but she was slotted into design.

Williams recalls paying her dues by drafting and doing the grunt work. "If you're young in your career," she says, "be a sponge and be willing to learn all you can." Facile and able to both draw well and build models quickly, she gained traction internally. She was invited to participate in higher-level design discussions, which proved to be a critical career boost.

Her time at SOM was hands-on. "You can't be this elite, effete designer, just drawing whatever you want and expecting somebody to clean it up for you," she says. "It's not just about the design component, it's about how it's put together, how you have to interface with the rest of the entities in the construction process, and understanding what a set of construction documents really do." She recalls going to building sites and watching contractors actually lay floor tile or set the joints that she designed in order to feel the connection between the documentation process and the execution in the field.

A career designer, Williams acknowledges the importance of the entire team. She says, "You can't live in a cocoon where all you're doing is designing and satisfying your own personal stuff." From 1980 to 1997, she worked for SOM in San Francisco, eventually becoming a senior associate partner. For a myriad of reasons, she realized she was probably never going to make partner, and knowing she wanted to lead and become well-rounded professionally, she began to consider other options.

A Washington, DC-based firm, Ai, approached her to open a San Francisco office—it was the perfect opportunity for her to take on a more encompassing role. Initially, she started working out of her husband Walter's closet with an old computer and some marketing counsel from her

DC partners. They told her to make a list of all her business contacts and break them down into classifications: the people who need to know you've moved on, the people who could bring business in the next five years, and those with immediate potential for work. She then began to reach out to these prospects.

With a reputation as a designer, Williams now had to learn management. And while she had colleagues in Washington, DC, who could help answer questions, she explains that California culture is very different from the Eastern seaboard. She learned how to develop fees, write contracts, staff an office, and even use Microsoft Excel, which is necessary for fee negotiations.

Williams found it was hard to wear both design and management hats because the shift from her left brain to right brain was tricky at times. During this period, Williams and Walter were raising two young boys. "I took work home or brought them to the office on weekends because I had a commitment to my family but also to make sure the company was profitable and that the work we were doing was as good as it could be," she says. "I had to do both, I had to figure out how to juggle it all."

When the dot-com bust occurred, it became more difficult to get projects. Williams noticed however that the jobs coming through the door were bigger, more durable projects as opposed to simple facilities for companies that might not be around tomorrow.

Perkins + Will, a large firm with a seventy-five-year history, approached Williams and her partners about an acquisition, which caused them to take pause. They had created a profitable company, but the world was changing, and medium-size firms—in her opinion—were in jeopardy. Williams and her partners were also in their fifties and liked the security a buyout would provide. Regardless, "the idea of retiring at sixty-five is ludicrous, because architecture is not the sort of thing you just turn off. It's something that is part of you forever," she says. "We had this great firm but it had reached a point where it needed something more, and we needed to make sure that we were part of something that had the potential for longevity."

They decided to sell Ai lock, stock, and barrel. In fact, everything became the property of Perkins and Will, including the projects, the rights to the work, even the liabilities. All partners signed employment agreements and had to stay with the new firm for three years. Williams has happily stayed longer—going on five years.

When asked if she considers herself a good businessperson now, Williams says simply, "I do." She doesn't want business as her daily responsibility, but she acknowledges that her experience running a company affects how she now approaches the design process. Elements such as knowledge of the client's background, the financial atmosphere in which you're trying to negotiate a contract, and the fees that you've decided on are all part of the information that impacts the relationship. "I want to see the fees even though I'm not responsible for negotiating," she says. "I want to make sure there's a compatible attitude about funding design. If a client doesn't want to pay for design, it's a red flag that it may not be a client you want to work with because we're a design firm and we want to make sure we're being invited to the table for projects where design is as high on the list of desirable outcomes as is profitability. You have to find that balance."

When pressed about how she pursues new business, Williams says, "It's about relationships—be it ongoing relationships with existing clients who want continuity or relationships that you've had with people through more casual interactions. Over time, these people get to know me and want to work together."

Due to the current economic climate, Williams realizes there's not as much work at this time—there's not as much capital to fund projects—so now it's about trying to find new angles and reaching out to different audiences.

Williams has never believed in formal mentoring programs but acknowledges, "Early on, there were at least a half dozen people who presented a portal for me to sort of poke my head through, gain understanding, and get some sense that there were no limits on what it was that I should or could do." She tried different things on for size, and while there were things that other people thought she shouldn't be doing, she persevered. "It's important to put yourself in places where you're not always comfortable. That's how you learn," she says. "Looking back, being female and black, I'm surprised by some of the things I've done, but at the time, it never occurred to me that I couldn't do them. I might make it easier for other women who see me succeeding without boundaries."

I asked Williams who her dream client would be. She knows immediately—a major cultural facility, museum, or a federal courthouse—citing that these significant projects are integral to the urban fabric. As for lessons learned, Williams suggests that seasoned architects constantly look for talented up-and-comers who are fifteen or twenty years their junior. They have new ideas, and both stand to learn a lot from the other. She also believes the first five years are critical to a new architect's career. She stresses the value in experiencing the whole process and says, "It doesn't take an iota away from their brilliance as designers. Actually, I think it makes them more broadly based, more responsible, and more innovative."

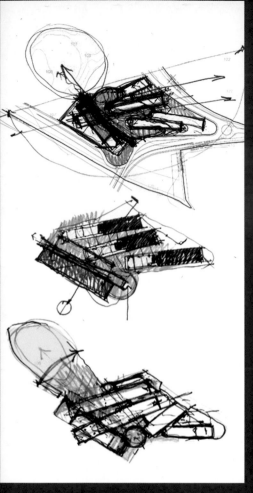

CREATE Research Park

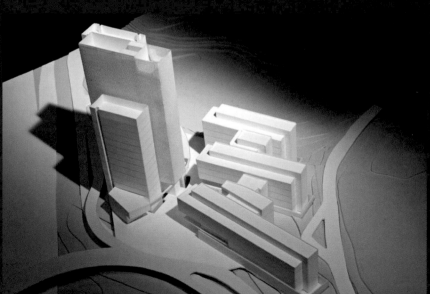

August Wilson Center
for African American Culture,
Pittsburg, PA
(Robert Mathewson/RENDIMAGE)

# About the Author

Jenn Kennedy is a writer and photographer. She contributes profiles and lifestyle content to a range of publications, including *Jane*, *Los Angeles Confidential*, *Las Vegas Magazine*, *Montecito Journal*, *Sierra*, *Out*, and *Fit Yoga*. She has shot campaigns and projects for corporations such as Citibank, Maytag, MTV, Yahoo!, Safeway, and Women's Entertainment Network. Kennedy has a weekly column on Noozhawk.com that profiles Santa Barbara business leaders; contributes business, lifestyle, and travel stories to shewired.com; blogs at kennedypens.com; and has a Web site of her photographs, kennedypix.com. She lives in Santa Barbara, California.